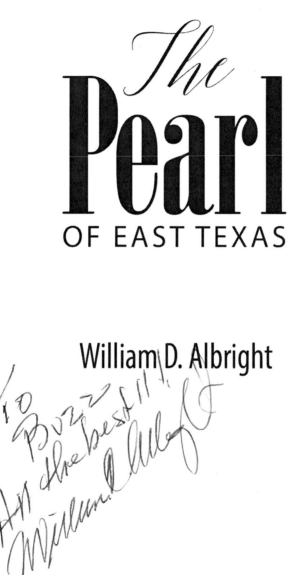

The Pearl

OF EAST TEXAS

William D. Albright

outskirtspress

DENVER, COLORADO

DEDICATION

Mom, because of your strength, I was inspired to pen this book.
I felt your story should not be confined only in the hearts of our family,
but shared by many others who chose to read about you.
May your story inspire others to be strong and courageous, and
make their mark on history. You are the "Pearl" in my heart.

To my daughters and grandchildren

And to Susie "Dennie" Dabner
Whose outstanding contributions
Made many of the sections of this book possible

Table of Contents

Prologue

Where is that hero to show us the way?
The one who will rise without fortune or fame
Where is that heroine to show us the light?
In the end we may not know her name

Excerpt from "The Hero Deep Within"
Copyright ©1991 by William D. Albright

On Tuesday 6 May 2003, the Berryville, Texas City Council held its monthly meeting at the city hall to discuss items pertinent to the city's income, safety, and overall prosperity. The meeting was attended by the mayor, council members, and fire chief, and was open to citizens who were interested in the affairs of the city. At this particular meeting the fire chief reported on his staff and the number of medical and fire calls responded to during the previous month, and one citizen suggested that Berryville sponsor a flea market as a means to raise income for the city. In addition, the mayor and several council members were officially sworn in, one council member was appointed Mayor Pro Tem, and a city ordinance on the control of rabies was discussed by the attendees, but was tabled for the June meeting. These were the types of items typically discussed at the council meetings.

The agenda could have also included the topic of condemning homes in the community, considered an important issue for the council to discuss. From time to time, houses have been abandoned or owners have died and their descendants have not wanted to have anything to do with the property. Keeping the city clean was a paramount objective of the council. In those instances where lots that have been overgrown with high grass and weeds, and where the city cannot locate the owners, the lots would be mowed to keep snakes and rodents from appearing, or tall grass from creating a potential fire hazard.

The council meets every month even when there is no pressing topic. Meetings are usually held the second Monday of each month at 6:30 p.m., and last from thirty minutes to two hours. Typically five citizens will attend a meeting in addition to the council members and the mayor, unless the agenda includes property taxes, and then the city hall is full. Occasionally, retiring council members and other officials are honored with a plaque and reception following the business portion of the meeting. Such was the case at the meeting on 6 May 2003 as Mattie Pearl Albright and Grace Donnelly were recognized for their many years of dedicated service to the city of Berryville. Each was presented with a plaque. This council meeting was held on a Tuesday, as the previous Saturday, May 3rd, was an election day for the city of Berryville, and Texas state law requires cities to swear in newly elected officials within a few days following an election.

Mattie and her husband, William D. Albright Sr., were aware that she was going to be honored on May 6th. At eighty-five years of age and in declining health, Mattie decided in 2002 to retire from the council. She had given up her Mayor Pro Tem responsibilities in 1996, but continued to serve on the city council. She had been requested by the mayor and council to attend the meeting to receive her totally justifiable and deserving recognition for officially serving the Berryville Community since the mid-1980s. Knowing that this meeting would be the last she would officially attend, she took the liberty of inviting family members and friends residing in the Berryville and Tyler, Texas areas to join her. She also desired to have her two sons, Gerald Anthony Albright and me, William D. Albright Jr. in attendance. When I received a phone call from Mom informing me of the meeting and requesting my attendance, I replied that I couldn't due to my corporate responsibilities. Needless to say, she was disappointed, but understood, as mothers do. However, immediately after hanging up, I telephoned Gerald to see if he could attend. He could. We would surprise her.

The morning of the next day, I contacted Sharyn Harrison, City Manager of Berryville, to inform her that Gerald and I would be attending the meeting, but wanted her to keep our arrival a secret. Sharyn gave her word, but since her feet were being held to the fire with a secret, she decided to return the favor by informing me that in addition to giving Mom the customary plaque for long service, the city was dedicating County Road (CR) 4117 as "Mattie Albright Road." Upon hearing this news, I choked with emotion, swore my secrecy, and contacted Gerald to inform him. Gerald too was thrilled, and exclaimed, "Wow, what an honor." Clearly, the council meeting on May 6th was not going to be an ordinary meeting, and Gerald and I were not going to miss the event.

The city of Shreveport, originally called Shreve Town, was founded in 1836 by a development corporation established to start a town where the Red River and the Texas Trail met. The Red River was cleared and made navigable by Captain Henry Miller Shreve, who commanded the United States Army Corps of Engineers at the time. Captain Shreve and his team cleared a huge logjam that had previously been an obstruction to the passage of ships on the river, and for this achievement, Shreve Town was named in his honor.

Shreve Town was originally contained within the boundaries of a section of land sold to the company by the indigenous Caddo Indians in the year 1835. In 1838, Shreve Town became the parish seat, equivalent to counties in other states, and was called Caddo Parish. On March 20, 1839, the town was incorporated as "Shreveport." Caddo and the surrounding parishes constituted the only region in Louisiana that was spared by the Civil War. Since the parish did not live through the terror, famine, and other sufferings brought on by the war, no reconstruction needed to be done there. Moreover, the war had brought great prosperity to the parish, as Shreveport became the capital of Confederate Louisiana after the fall of New Orleans in the spring of 1862. In fact, Jefferson Davis, President of the Confederate

States of America, attempted to flee to Shreveport when he left Richmond, Virginia in 1865 at the end of the war. He was captured on May 10, 1865 in Irwinville, Georgia.

Since the northwest region of Louisiana escaped invasion and was occupied only after the surrender of the southern armies, white people there did not feel they had been defeated. As a consequence, the white community in Caddo Parish was periodically dominated by men who greatly opposed the federal government and its reconstruction policies, and who strongly resented the presence of federal troops, particularly when those occupying forces were composed of black regiments. These men stubbornly resisted the changes brought on as a result of the victory by the Union forces, and did not shrink from taking any action, including committing murder. Violence, consequently, became the ultimate instrument in attempting to coerce blacks into submission and in maintaining Caddo as a white man's country. There were numerous homicides in Caddo in the decade following the Civil War, giving the parish its nickname: "Bloody Caddo." Violence toward African-Americans was highly organized and often occurred en masse. It wasn't until January 29, 1876 that the Federal forces, including black troops, were withdrawn.

The end of the Civil War, however, also brought the beginnings of civil and political freedom to African-Americans in Louisiana and particularly Shreveport. Blacks were given the right to vote and serve on juries as a result of the Thirteenth and Fourteenth Amendments, and in 1865, the Freedmen's Bureau assisted former slaves in Caddo Parish to secure fair-paying jobs, medical care, and education; they established elementary schools for black children; and they negotiated labor contracts with former slave-owners. Finally, the earliest civil rights campaign of the Reconstruction era in the South occurred in Louisiana.

Most of the southern states affected by the Civil War began to recover during the period of Reconstruction that lasted from 1863, following the Emancipation Proclamation, to 1877. According to history books, the first railroad in Shreveport was completed in 1866, and the city became the hub of railroad transportation, as it gave access to Dallas, Texas; Little Rock, Arkansas; and St. Louis, Missouri. The Vicksburg, Shreveport, & Pacific Railroad built a bridge across the Red River at Cotton Street that gave access to the East. Trains also ran from Shreveport to New Orleans. Construction of the railroad spawned sawmills for the milling of crossties and other elements for bridge construction. Lumber became an economic mainstay alongside cotton. In time, the railroads provided a suitable alternative to shipping up and down the Red River, and the shipping industry began to decline.

Starting with the Reconstruction years, new and better buildings were erected, and new suburbs were developed at the western edge of the city. When the Shreveport City Railroad Company laid the first mule-drawn streetcar lines in 1870, it ran along Texas Street, Common Street, and Texas Avenue to the community boundaries. Shreveport became an industrial city with sawmills, planing mills, foundries, a plant making cotton gins, and a cottonseed oil mill, among others. In 1890 a commercial electric streetcar trolley system, the first of its kind in the state, began operating in Shreveport. It became convenient to live on the outskirts of town and commute to work. Also in that year the fire department became professional and tapped a new water supply, allowing the department to be more effective in fighting fires. The downtown streets were paved, starting in 1897, but did not reach many neighborhoods until years later. Because lumber was a major industry for the city, many homes were made entirely of wood. This was particularly true in the black neighborhoods where inhabitants resided in both project developments as well as neighborhoods comprised of single-family homes. The latter had yards around them that served as playgrounds for black children. In many cases, the yards provided some room to plant vegetable gardens to grow food for the family, and flowers to beautify the houses.

In the early 1900s, middle-class blacks primarily lived in the Lakeside and Allendale communities of Shreveport in single-family homes. Most middle-class whites lived in the Queensborough section nearby. There was also a community called St. Paul's Bottoms that served as the red-light district of Shreveport, and featured saloons, brothels, and dance halls. The blues singer and guitarist Huddie William Ledbetter, commonly known as "Lead Belly," and other jazz and ragtime artists shared their skills in The Bottoms. Poorer blacks and whites lived side by side in this community.

Jim Crow laws were very much alive in the South during Reconstruction and the decades that followed, and Louisiana and the city of Shreveport were no exception. Blacks could utilize the public transportation that was available in the city, but they were required to ride in the back of trolleys and buses. Blacks could shop in the department stores, but could not try on clothes. There were separate restrooms and water fountains for blacks in department stores and restaurants, if they were able to enter at all. Black children also had no public elementary or high schools to attend, except for those held in local churches and homes. They had to buy their books and school supplies, since no support was provided by the state for these items. This lasted for many years until Julius Rosenwald, influenced by Booker T. Washington, established the Rosenwald Fund that financed over five thousand "Rosenwald Schools" in the United States, which were built primarily for the education of blacks in the early 20th century. Rosenwald was an American clothier who became part-owner and president of Sears, Roebuck and Company. He was the founder of the "Fund" and contributed seed money for many of the schools and other philanthropic causes. Around 1923 in Shreveport, an elementary school was built to support students up to grade seven, and eventually, a high school was established to take students through the twelfth grade. Despite Rosenwald's matching donations toward the construction of these and other black schools in the US, by the mid-1930s, white schools in the South were funded over five times more per student than black schools.

It was illegal for blacks to learn to read and write in the south during slavery. Even after they were "emancipated" by President Lincoln in 1863, illiteracy continued to dominate during Reconstruction and the implementation of Jim Crow. Illiteracy among blacks as well as poor whites in Louisiana began to lessen following the election of Huey P. Long as governor of the state in 1928, and as senator in 1932. Long had a genuine concern for the common people of Louisiana, both black and white. He remodeled the school system to enable eight-month terms to be maintained in the poorest parishes and provided free textbooks. He strongly supported the Julius Rosenwald campaign against illiteracy, and 100,000 adults in Louisiana, white and black, learned to read and write in his first term as governor. He expanded funding for Louisiana State University, tripled its enrollment, lowered tuition, and established scholarships for low-income students. With respect to other infrastructure programs, and though he had much opposition, Long's public works program for Louisiana was unprecedented in the South. During his four years as governor, he increased paved highways in Louisiana from a few hundred miles to several thousand miles. By 1936, the infrastructure program begun by Long had completed some 9700 miles of new roads, doubling the size of the state's road system. He built 111 bridges, including one over the Red River in Shreveport, and started construction on the first bridge over the Mississippi River. Prior to this, residents had to take ferries to cross the rivers. He built a new governor's mansion and a new Louisiana State Capitol, at the time the tallest building in the South. All of these projects provided thousands of much-needed jobs during the Great Depression, including ten percent of the nation's highway workers. Huey Long was assassinated in 1935 at the age of forty-two.

The Jim Crow South was the environment that welcomed Mattie Pearl Dabner on 1 September 1917. She was born with the assistance of a midwife by the name of Amelia Williams. She became the third and last child born to the 1912 union of George Archie Dabner, Sr. and Mary Ward Dabner. Their first two children were sons and the arrival of Mattie gave them the daughter they wished for to round out the structure of the family. Mattie's older brothers were George Archie Dabner Jr. born 5 October 1912, and Cornelius Clifton Dabner, born 30 July 1915. As was customary in many families in the South, where children are named after others in the family, George was named after his father, Cornelius was named after his father's sister, Cornelia, and Mattie was named after her father's older sister Mattie Hill Dabner, and her mother's younger sister Martha Mattie Rosetta Ward. The origin of the "Pearl" part of Mattie's name is unknown, but given what she eventually gave to her family and the communities in which she lived, it was clearly appropriate for this precious jewel to be part of her moniker.

The Dabner family is of both African and Native American descent, and George Sr. and Mary, both born in Louisiana, actually met in Muskogee City, Oklahoma. George Sr., Mom's father, was born on March 3, 1886. He was the son of Archie Dabner, born in 1858, and Mary Hill, both born in Texas. They had seven children: Mattie, born October 1883; Duncan, born July 1885; George (Mom's father), born March 1886; Cornelia, born April 1888; Hattie, born February 1890; Samuel Alford, born January 1893; and Henry, born October 1893. They were all born in Shreveport or nearby cities in Louisiana, following the marriage of Archie and Mary on October 21, 1880 in Ouachita, Louisiana. Mom's father, George, started working at an early age as a porter for the Bernstein Brothers on Murphy Street in Shreveport in the early 1900s. The brothers owned a grocery, drug, and general merchandise business. One of the brothers, Ernest R. Bernstein, was also a bank vice president and later, Mayor of Shreveport.

Archie Dabner, George's father, was originally born Archie Hill, son of Randall and Lucy Ann Hill, both born in Georgia. They were part of the movement to relocate workers from the older eastern states to newer cotton-growing states in the west such as Texas. In 1860, Randall, Lucy Ann, and young Archie were slaves for a white farmer in Canton, Smith County, Texas. Unfortunately, Randall ended up in the penitentiary for stealing, and after some years had gone by, Lucy decided to get a divorce. Her second marriage was to Jerry Dabner, and the entire family including Archie's two sisters, Cornelia and Serena, took his last name. Like Archie, Cornelia and Serena were born in Texas, in 1863 and 1864, respectively.

In the early 1900s, the Archie Dabner family, including George and his six siblings, was residing in Louisiana. Reportedly, Archie or his stepfather Jerry killed a white man following an altercation. Given the times in the South, it was decided that George and his brothers and sisters needed to leave Louisiana, at least temporarily. George moved to Muskogee, Oklahoma, and his brothers Duncan and Sam relocated to Texas. George worked as a servant for a family in Muskogee from 1910 through 1913, and began developing his craft as a tailor. And there, he also met Mary Ward, and married her in early 1912.

Mary Ward, Mom's mother, was born December 28, 1889 in Shreveport. Her genealogical history begins with her grandparents, Tom Johnson Hodge (Harjo), born in 1820 in Georgia, and Hannah Hodge (Harjo), born 1820 in Alabama. From this union, three children were born including Green Hodge (Harjo) (1836); Johnson Hodge (Harjo) (1837); and Delia Hodge (Harjo) (1839). The term "Harjo" is the Creek Nation family name for Hodge. Johnson Hodge's Creek Nation name is Hillabee Harjo. "Hillabee" referred to a complex of towns and villages in east central Alabama. Creeks were a matriarchal society and culture, and the mother town of the villages was called Hillabee. Following the marriage of Johnson to his wife Margaret (Maggie), they produced a large family with approximately fifteen offspring between 1863 and 1888. All of these children except one were born in Texas.

One of these individuals was Laura Hodge (Harjo), born in 1868 with her twin sister, Nettie Hodge (Harjo). Laura married Mathias (Mathew) William Ward, also from Texas, and to this union, seven children were born: J. Thomas Ward, born 1888; Mary Ward (Mom's mother), born 1889; Monroe Ward, born

1891; Markham Ward, born 1892; Daniel Ward, born 1893; Henry Charles Ward, born 1894; and Martha Mattie Rosetta Ward, born 1896. All were born in Louisiana with the exception of Daniel, who was born in Okmulgee, Oklahoma. Laura's oldest sister, Effie Hodge (Harjo) born in 1863, married Edward Ward, the unconfirmed brother of Mathew William Ward. This union produced one child, Charley Ward, born in August 1883 in Texas. Besides being a farmer for most of his life, legend has it that Charley testified before Congress regarding land rights for Native Americans. He died June 15th, 1970 in Okmulgee, the capital of the Muscogee (Creek) Nation since the United States Civil War.

As previously noted, Laura's family was originally from Alabama, and she, her parents and siblings all received payment made to those Creeks who were removed from Alabama and other southeastern states and sent to the Indian Territories in Oklahoma as part of the "Trail of Tears." In accordance with the 12th Article of the Treaty of 1832, their removal was at the expense of the United States, and they were to "receive subsistence while upon the journey, and for one year after their arrival at their new homes." This treaty was one of several made with the "Five Civilized Tribes" between 1814 and 1832. As one of the Five Civilized Tribes, the Creek had gradually ceded lands under pressure from European-American settlers and the US government. President Andrew Jackson signed the Indian Removal Act in 1830, which ultimately led to the deportation of native peoples in the southeast to the Indian Territories west of the Mississippi River, mostly in Oklahoma and Texas.

Following the death of Laura in the early 1900s, Mary Ward was sent to the reservation of the Creek Nation in Muskogee, Oklahoma. She was living on Ellsworth Avenue. There she met and eventually married George Dabner in 1912. Although the Reconstruction reforms in Louisiana continued to be met with harsh and violent resistance from some whites in Caddo Parish, the fact that the reforms were in place created the potential for more employment opportunities and stability for the predominant and robust population of blacks in the city. Moreover, Shreveport was "home" to George and Mary, and they decided to move back there with young George, Jr. in 1914. George, Jr. had been born in October 1912 in Muskogee. Within the next three years, Clifton and Mom were brought into the world, in 1915 and 1917, respectively. For the first few years after returning to Shreveport, Mary was a homemaker, talking care of her three young offspring.

The fact that they were living in the southern state of Louisiana, and were of African and Native American descent, incentivized George and Mary to work diligently, develop job-related and life skills, forge a close relationship with others in the Dabner and Ward families in Shreveport, and provide a positive environment for their children, making certain that they were ethical, disciplined, and educated. Survival was the order of the day. The plan was clearly being implemented when tragedy hit the family on 4 July 1920, as George, Sr. passed away from malaria at the age of thirty-seven. At the time of his death, George Jr. was almost eight, Clifton was five, and Mom was almost three. Mary, who came to be known in the family as "Mother Dear" and "Nana," now had the responsibility to raise her three young children by herself, with support from her extended family. She was a homemaker and had not worked in Shreveport while her husband George was living, since he was bringing in sufficient income at the time to take care of the family. He was employed in a regular blue-collar job, was a tailor on the side, and earned income as a gospel singer in a group. Congregations at churches where he and his group of five sang would contribute a little more to the church offerings to provide the group with a donation.

At the time, George and Mary were purchasing a home in the Lakeside community of Shreveport on Ashton Street—a three-bedroom dwelling made of wood, like most houses. The home was in a nice community of fellow black occupants, had a yard where Mom and her brothers could play, and enough room to plant a vegetable garden. It had running water in the kitchen and an in-house toilet. There was no bathtub with running water, however, and baths had to be taken in a large galvanized tin tub, with water drawn from the kitchen sink or the well. While times were very hard in the 1920s, the family was surviving, and doing a little better than many by comparison. When the city decided to implement Huey Long's plan to pave neighborhood streets like it had done in the downtown area, it required homeowners to pay an additional fee to finance this particular civic improvement. Mother Dear found this additional cost insurmountable, and eventually, the house was lost and the family relocated to a nearby home they rented on Weinstock Street, the next street over from Ashton Street.

Mother Dear surely knew what it meant to be independent and a survivor. This was important because over the next two decades the United States would face some major challenges including droughts, race riots, Jim Crow laws, and the stock market crash and subsequent depression. The family lore handed down over the years was that Mother Dear was strong in her convictions and determination. She began working and continued to develop her craft as a shirt finisher, presser, and domestic. Though the family didn't have much, she did whatever was ethically possible to ensure the survival of the family. All worked hard, took care of their individual responsibilities, maintained good hygiene, and had a strong family bond. Over the years Mom would tell the story that Mother Dear had two dresses to wear during the work week, and washed and ironed one every night to ensure it was ready when she went to work. The independence, hard work, discipline, and strength shown by Mother Dear greatly impressed her young daughter as she transitioned from being a little girl to becoming a teenager, and then an adult. These behaviors would be further enhanced by the relationship she had with her older brother, George Jr., who took it upon himself to be the "head of the household" and "surrogate father" over Mom. She resisted this, and her pursuit to be independent and her own woman like her mother competed with George's attempt to control her. This sibling rivalry placed a strain on their relationship for many years.

Conversely, Mom had a very close and respectful relationship with Clifton, whom she revered as her true big brother. He protected her, and taught her to drive. He was pulled out of school by Mother Dear to go to work and earn money to help the family make ends meet. This caused a rift in the extended Dabner family, as a number of members felt that George, Jr., as the oldest, should work to support the family. Mother Dear, however, had made her decision, and as a result, Clifton never graduated from high school. He bought a new bicycle and made deliveries for drug stores and other businesses. He also worked as a shoe shine man and hotel porter. He and his brother George were avid golfers, and Clifton made additional money on the weekend serving as a caddie. He was responsible, and also practiced his professions and those of his mother as the stories and early pictures show him as well-groomed and immaculately dressed, with shoes shining like glass. Because of the role he played, Mom saw Clifton not only as her brother but also someone she admired. They were very close.

In 1931, George, Jr. graduated from Central Colored (CC) High School, the first and only public high school for African-American children at the time in Shreveport. The school was founded in 1917. In 1934, he married Mabel Bates, one of twelve children that her parents, a white man and black woman, brought into the world. Since the Bates had a racially mixed marriage, they were not allowed to cohabitate in Louisiana. As such, they lived next door to each other on Garden Street in two homes Mr. Bates was able to purchase as the owner of a successful dairy. As time passed, the Bates eventually moved into one of the homes, since a number of children had grown up and moved on. More importantly, blacks and whites were allowed to marry and cohabitate, under the leadership of Huey Long.

George and Mabel were actually married one year before they

told their respective families. When Mabel's father became aware of the union, he wanted to put a contract killing out on George, as he didn't like him and Mabel was still in high school. He forced Mabel out of the home, telling her he did not want to see her again. She was disowned by the family. Mabel and George lived with Mother Dear and family on Weinstock Street. Mabel never saw her father alive again. When the Bates family informed her of what turned out to be her father's fatal illness in the mid-1940s, she decided to take the train from Philadelphia to Shreveport to see him. He died while she was in transit. George and Mabel were married for sixty-nine years. They had twins who were stillborn.

Susie Virginia Lyles met mom in the second grade at Ingersoll Elementary School, lived in the Lakeside community, and in 1930, entered the eighth grade at CC High with Mom. They graduated together in 1934 in a class of 102 students. One of Susie's sisters, Katie, had a difficult time pronouncing Susie's middle name, Virginia, when she was small, and would enunciate it as "Dennie." This name stuck, and Susie has been referred to as "Dennie" by the family and close friends. She married Mom's brother Clifton in 1936. Dennie shared that Clifton always looked good whether he was wearing his crisp ironed jeans or one of several custom-made suits. But he had no money. When they were married, Clifton had only his clothes, which prompted Dennie to decide to take care of the family's finances. They were married for sixty-seven years and to this union, six children were born: Twins Clifton Jr. who lived for one day, and Faye who lived for a little over a month in 1937; Mary Virginia born in 1938; George III in 1939; Wendell in 1940; and Linda

Pearl (named after Mattie Pearl) in 1942. The family lived in a rented house on Anna Street in Shreveport.

According to Dennie, "Mattie was a leader and was involved in and headed up a number of programs at the school. She also sang in the chorus and played basketball for CC High. Mattie's popularity on the campus and in the community was very high, and this took the spotlight away from her brother George, further straining their relationship." Mom also sang soprano in the choir at Antioch Baptist Church. Founded in 1866, the church is the oldest African-American Baptist congregation in Shreveport, and it not only served as a place to worship, but was also the center of gravity for the community to discuss the civic, cultural, and political issues of the day. The influences of Mother Dear and Mom's experiences at CC High and Antioch helped to shape some of her fundamental beliefs about the need to be assertive, confident, compassionate toward others, and collaborative in working with colleagues to achieve goals. She was on her way, and like Captain Henry Shreve, she would eliminate some of the logjams that existed in the communities where she lived or take them to new heights in terms of economic development and prosperity.

Shortly after graduating from high school, mom married Alonzo Simon on 23 December 1934. A good friend of Clifton, and liked by the Dabner family, Alonzo also worked as a shoe shine man in the local barbershops and as a presser in a cleaners/laundry. Clearly working in the laundry, tailoring, and cleaning business was a common occupation for the Dabner/Lyle clan, and this would be realized in the future. During Reconstruction and the early parts of the twentieth century, few blacks occupied "professional" jobs. Most worked on farms, in factories or cleaners, or worked as domestics. Those who were able to attend one of the historically black colleges were trained to be primarily teachers or preachers.

Mom and Alonzo lived with Mother Dear on Weinstock Street in Shreveport for eight years following their marriage in 1934. In early 1937 Mom became pregnant and later that year Mary Cornelius Simon was delivered stillborn. Though she did not survive, the naming of an infant after others in the family was in force and Mary Cornelius was named after several of mom's favorite people at the time—her mother and paternal grandmother, both named Mary, her brother Clifton, whose first name was Cornelius, and her favorite Aunt Cornelia, her father's sister.

Map of Shreveport in 1920

→ Weinstock Street

★ Central Colored High School

★ Antioch Baptist Church

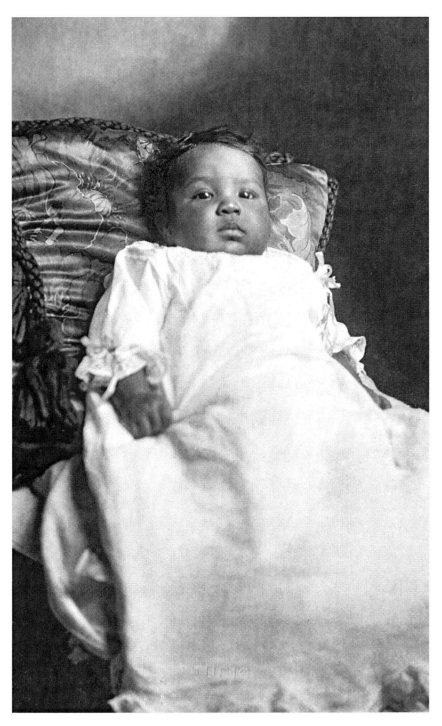

Mattie Pearl Dabner in Christening Gown in 1917

George Jr., Clifton, Mattie Pearl and Mary W. Dabner (Mother Dear) in Front of Their Home on Ashton St. in Shreveport—circa 1920

Mattie Pearl Dabner at Easter—circa 1920

George A. Dabner, Father of Mattie Pearl Dabner and Husband to Mary Dabner—circa 1917

Mary W. Dabner (Mother Dear) circa 1935

Mattie Pearl as a High School Beauty—circa 1934

Mattie Is Ready to Take on the World—circa 1937

Mattie Strolling Down the Avenue in Shreveport—circa 1939

Antioch Baptist Church—Shreveport, Louisiana

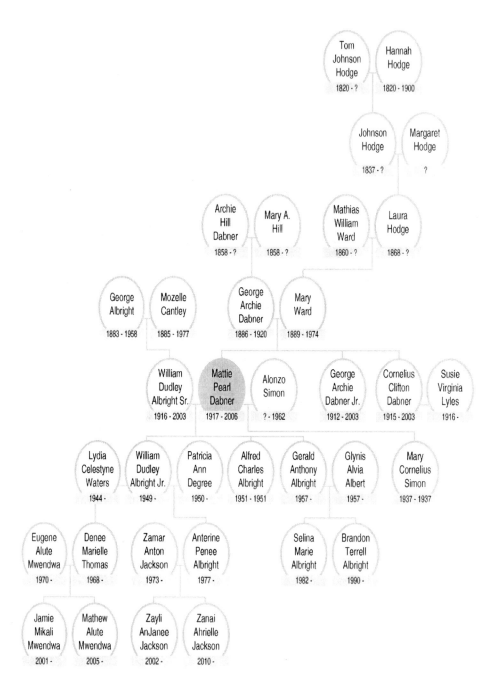

THE DABNER/WARD FAMILY TREE

The onset of World War II and the involvement of the United States as a result of the bombing of Pearl Harbor in December 1941 presented an opportunity for the Dabner family to reassess where the family should reside. Mom's brother George and his wife Mabel had already relocated to the East Coast in 1938 and were living in Haddonville, New Jersey. George found employment with assistance from Aunt Hattie Dabner, one of his father's sisters. He eventually became a tailor, following in the footsteps of his father. The family still living in Shreveport including Mother Dear, Clifton and family, and Mom and Alonzo were determining the best course of action to take. Though Shreveport was home to the Dabners, it was time to move on as employment opportunities had become limited, Jim Crow laws were still being enforced, and racially oriented upheavals were very prevalent. Clifton, as a family man, had been given a choice regarding serving in the military—either join the army, or work for an industry that was supporting the country's war effort. For the latter option, he could have worked in either Chicago or Philadelphia. Since George Jr. was already living on the East Coast in nearby Haddonville, New Jersey, Clifton chose to work in Philadelphia. He relocated first in 1943 and found employment at Midville Steel and was making parts for military vehicles to support the war. Six months later Mother Dear, Dennie, and her four children took a train operated by the Southern Pacific Railroad Company from Shreveport to St. Louis, where they changed trains and rode on to Philadelphia. It took a total of three days and nights to reach their final destination. Since the country was at war, transporting troops took precedence over civilians taking trains. Because of this, the Dabner family had to leave the train three times while en route to allow the troops to board. The first was in Louisiana, and they had to spend the night in St. Louis due to troop movement. Once the family arrived in Philadelphia, as well as their furniture that had been relocated from Shreveport to Philadelphia by moving van, George and Mabel moved from Haddonville to Philadelphia to join the family. Later in 1943, George was drafted into the United States Marine Corps, and served for five years primarily in Japan and China during and after World War II.

Because of the war, defense-related production was booming and the car, steel, rubber, and housing industries were in high gear on the West Coast, and particularly in Los Angeles. Being an independent soul, Mom was convinced that opportunities were better in the western part of the country, and the weather was more to her liking. And so she and Alonzo decided to leave Mother Dear's household in 1942 and relocate to Los Angeles. Alonzo was the first to relocate to Los Angeles by traveling with friends, and Mom followed shortly thereafter by train. They became part of the second large migration of blacks from southern states like Louisiana and Texas to escape racial violence and seek better employment and other opportunities in cities like Los Angeles. The first wave occurred in the 1920s for the same reasons, but the population relocated to both California (primarily Los Angeles) and northern states like Michigan, Illinois, and Indiana to work in the automotive and other industries. There was a slowdown in migration between the two waves, primarily because of the stock market crash and the subsequent depression, and those giving thought to relocating decided to remain where they were until the environment improved. Many of those who relocated during the first migration and the early part of the second traveled by carpooling if they were fortunate, while others hopped freight trains. This practice became very popular among migrant workers or "hobos" who were unable to afford other means of transportation especially during the Great Depression.

In 1942, Mom was able to purchase a ticket to take the Sunset Limited passenger train operated by the Southern Pacific Railroad Company. Thousands of individuals desiring to leave Louisiana and Texas and move to the West Coast took the Sunset Limited. As a child, I was given a train set that was a replica of the train Mom rode to Los Angeles to commemorate this important transition in her life. When I was six months old, I took the Sunset Limited back to East Texas with my parents for the funeral of my father's grandmother, Anna Cantley Payne, wife of John Cantley. She passed away on May 28, 1950.

Most wars bring about major business opportunities for companies that can support the war effort, and this was surely the case for such companies in the Los Angeles (LA) and surrounding areas. By the time the Simons arrived in LA in 1942, many blacks who settled there in the 1920s were able to use their skills acquired from working on the farms of the South to obtain blue-collar jobs as custodians, lumber haulers, brick layers, ditch diggers, etc. Over time, these workers moved into nicer apartments and eventually saved enough money to put a down payment on a home.

The Simons concluded they made the correct decision in relocating to Los Angeles and shortly after moving there, began operating a dry cleaner owned by a white couple on Fair Oaks Avenue in Pasadena, a suburb city just north of LA. They were continuing to practice the crafts and skills attained in Shreveport. They both handled the cleaning aspects, but Mom took care of the business requirements (bookkeeping, banking, taxes, etc.) of the operation. For the first few months, business prospects appeared promising, but Alonzo's behavior began to change. While Mom was enjoying the environment in Los Angeles, Alonzo's transition from Shreveport to Los Angeles was much more difficult. He began drinking heavily and spending money recklessly. Mom made the decision that the marriage had to end, and she filed for and was granted a divorce in early 1943. The dry cleaning venture was terminated. Following the divorce, Alonzo joined the army in 1945. He died in Shreveport in 1962.

After divorcing Alonzo, Mom re-established close ties with her Aunt Mattie, (Mother Dear's sister) for whom she was named, and her five children; Dorrice, Kathryn, Bessie, Benjamin, and Fannie. The family name was Shepherd from Aunt Mattie's marriage to a gentleman with this surname. Aunt Mattie and family moved from Shreveport to Los Angeles in the 1940 – 1941 timeframe. Mom also worked and socialized with friends, including two who relocated from Shreveport to Los Angeles and attended CC High: Mattie Bell James, who became one of my two godmothers, and Geneva Taylor, who later became Geneva Smith after she married.

At age twenty-six, Mom was a divorcee and in her prime. One evening in early 1943, she and Geneva were at a club located on Central Avenue in the South Central section of Los Angeles that housed a number of social venues for blacks in the 1940s. While at the club she met William D. Albright, a handsome 27-year-old gentleman, who had enlisted in the Army in February 1943 at Fort MacArthur in San Pedro, California. There was an immediate attraction, and they began to date. Several months later on 19 September 1943, they were married at Fort Bliss, Texas. Mom traveled with her new husband while he was assigned to various army posts over the next three years. These included Fort Bliss, where they were married; the Signal Corps Photo Center in Long Island, New York; Fort Myers, Florida; and Philadelphia, Pennsylvania. She enjoyed traveling and seeing other parts of the country. They were fortunately able to stay together, as William was never assigned to combat duty overseas during World War II, but was kept stateside as a photo laboratory technician, the profession for which he was trained while in Long Island.

When Mom was asked how William proposed marriage, she responded by saying that it wasn't a proposal at all but rather a declaration: "I guess you know that we are getting married," he said. Also, given the times and the lack of money, William didn't give Mom a wedding ring. This deficiency on his part was corrected many years later. However, Mom was concerned about not having a ring on her finger while living on army bases. At five foot seven inches tall, she was a striking woman who resembled both of her parents and carried physical features from her African-American and Creek ancestries. She had black wavy hair, a medium-brown complexion, and was lighter in color than her parents—one never knew how a child from mixed heritages would turn out. Being a resourceful and independent individual, she scraped enough money together to purchase a ring from a pawn shop that she wore with pride. The ring helped to keep soldiers at bay. This ring was bequeathed to her granddaughter, Anterine Penee Albright Jackson, following Mom's passing in March 2006.

Staff Sergeant William Albright completed his three-year obligation to the army, and was honorably discharged in February 1946. He departed the armed services by being processed through the Separation Center at Camp Beale, California near Sacramento. He and Mom decided to settle back in Los Angeles, as they concluded that the city appeared to provide the best opportunities for employment and they loved the environment the city offered to raise a family. They lived in temporary housing and with friends while searching for permanent housing. William secured full-time employment with the United States Post Office at the Terminal Annex in Los Angeles in 1946, and later, supplemented that income with part-time employment at the Automobile Club of Southern California. Mom obtained employment with the Bell Telephone Company.

They were also attempting to start a family, which was proving difficult. Mom lost one child, Mary Cornelius Simon, when married to her first husband, and becoming pregnant with William was becoming a challenge. After trying for several years, they reached the conclusion that bringing a child into the world would not occur, and made plans to use some of the money they saved to purchase a new car and drive around the western parts of the United States and Canada during the summer of 1949. Seeing several of the national parks like Yosemite, Bryce, and Kings Canyons and the Dakotas were desired points of interest. They purchased a '49 Plymouth Deluxe in the spring and began to develop the trip itinerary. Mom also visited Dr. Taylor, her obstetrician, as she had missed a menstrual cycle. His first name must have been "Doctor," as everyone called him Dr. Taylor. He was from Shreveport and while there, he was the obstetrician for the Dabner family. He delivered Mary Cornelius Simon, who was stillborn, and all six of the children born to Clifton and Susie Dabner. He moved to Los Angeles in the mid-1940s and set up his practice. On that spring day in 1949, Dr. Taylor informed Mom that she was indeed pregnant, and given her medical history, needed to cancel the planned road trip.

Advertising poster for the Sunset Limited, operated by Southern Pacific Lines, the passenger train Mattie took from Louisiana to Los Angeles in 1942

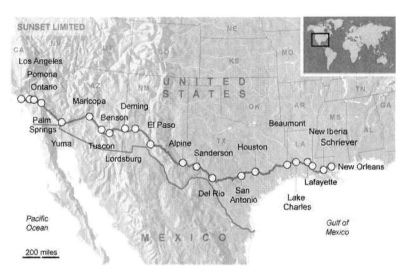

The route taken by the Sunset Limited between New Orleans and
Los Angeles

Mr. and Mrs. William D Albright—circa 1943

Mr. and Mrs. William D Albright—circa 1947

William and Mattie Albright with New 1949 Plymouth Deluxe

From its unique history, Los Angeles changed rapidly after 1848, when California was transferred to the United States as a result of the Treaty of Guadalupe Hidalgo that ended the Mexican-American War. The completion of the Transcontinental Railroad in 1876 really opened up the western part of the country, and as a result, "The West" experienced tremendous growth in population and in diversity. This diversity also brought about violent ethnic and class conflict, reflected in the struggle over who would control the identity, image, geography, and history of Los Angeles.

The city had only 2100 black Americans in 1900, according to census figures. By 1920 this grew to approximately 15,000. In 1910, the city had the highest percentage of black home ownership in the nation, with more than 36 percent of the city's African-American residents owning their own homes. Even with the periodic racial conflicts, the city was deemed a haven for blacks since they were less subjected to racial discrimination due to their population being small and the ongoing tensions between whites (Anglos) and Mexicans. That changed in the 1920s when restrictive covenants that enforced segregation in housing became widespread. Blacks were mostly confined along the South Central corridor of Watts, and small enclaves in Venice and Pacoima, which according to history, received far fewer services than other parts of the city. After World War II, the city's black population grew from 63,774 in 1940 to 170,000 a decade later as many continued to flee from the South with the hope for less racially oriented violence, better employment opportunities, and more respect in general. By 1960, Los Angeles had the fifth-largest black population in the United States, larger than any city in the South. Even though the Supreme Court banned the legal enforcement of race-oriented restrictive covenants in 1948, blacks remained in segregated enclaves.

The area known as Watts is a 2.12 square-mile neighborhood in Los Angeles, located on the Rancho La Tajauta Mexican land grant of 1843. As on all "ranchos," the principal vocation at that time was grazing and beef production. With the influx of European American settlers into Southern California in the 1870s, La Tajuata land was sold off and subdivided for smaller farms and homes, including a 220-acre parcel purchased by Charles H. Watts in 1886 for alfalfa and livestock farming. In those days each La Tajuata farm had an artesian well, an underground water reservoir under positive pressure, with those closer to the surface more likely to be used for water supply and irrigation.

The arrival of the transcontinental railroad spurred the settlement and development of the Los Angeles area. Most of the first residents were the "traqueros," Mexican and Mexican American rail workers who constructed and maintained the new rail lines. With this new growth, Watts was initially incorporated as a separate city, but later voted to annex itself to Los

Angeles in 1926. The community and its railroad station, Watts Station, took their names from the Watts family who donated the acreage for their establishment. The Station, built in 1904, was one of a number of stations where the "Red Car," operated by Pacific Electric Railway, stopped to pick up passengers who traveled between the city of Long Beach and downtown Los Angeles. During the 1930s through the 1950s, many citizens of Watts boarded these electric trains to shop downtown, eat at restaurants, and see movies. The train provided the residents of Watts and other nearby communities with additional options to shop rather than totally depending on patronizing local vendors. This was particularly important if one didn't have a car, given the sprawling makeup of the city of Los Angeles. This was also many years before the establishment of "malls" that housed many stores and other activities in one facility.

Watts did not become predominantly black until the 1940s. Before then, there were some black residents, many of whom were Pullman car porters and cooks. By 1914, a black realtor, Charles C. Leake, was doing business in the area, and marketing it as a community in which blacks should settle. During World War II, the city built several large housing projects including Hacienda Village, Nickerson Gardens, Jordan Downs, and Imperial Courts for the thousands of new workers employed in the various industries supporting the war. By the early 1960s, these projects had become nearly 100 percent black, as whites moved on to new suburbs outside the central city of Los Angeles. As industrial jobs disappeared from the area due to the end of the war, the projects housed many more poor families than they had previously.

Mom and Dad had already determined that the Los Angeles area was where they wanted to settle, work, and hopefully raise a family. And as it turned out, the Watts community of Los Angeles was where the Albright family was to spend the next two and a half decades.

Los Angeles, CA and surrounding areas

Looking east down Main Street of Watts (later to become 103rd St.) in 1912

Watts Station, one of the depots for the Red Car. Circa 1942

The Red Car Operated by Pacific Electric Railway. The car traveled between Long Beach and Downtown Los Angeles, with a stop in the Community of Watts

The Watts Towers, *the most recognizable monument of Watts, built by architect Simon Rodia from Italy between 1921 and 1954.*

David Starr Jordan High School located on 103rd Street was the primary public high school for residents living in Watts

Chapter 5
Family Life

The dream of Mattie Pearl Albright to have children finally came true on 1 December 1949 when Dr. Taylor helped her to deliver an 8 pound 6 ounce baby boy. She and her husband William decided to name their new son William Dudley Albright Jr., in keeping with the family tradition of naming children after close relatives. But the proud father wanted to ensure that his son was referred to by his given first name or an associated nickname, and not "Junior." As such, and as I grew, I was also known as Billy or Bill.

A few months after I was born, and with the support of the mortgage insurance program sponsored by the Federal Housing Administration (FHA), Dad and Mom purchased their first home, at 1329 East 104th Street in the Los Angeles community of Watts. They were fortunate to obtain a loan from the FHA, as many blacks across the nation were denied loans from this federal agency. One factor for receiving it may have been that the house was located in the South Central community of Watts, one of the few enclaves where blacks were allowed to buy in Los Angeles. De facto-segregation in housing, and the fall-out effect this had on education, was alive and well in the North and West, and, as Martin Luther King stated, "was as injurious to blacks as the actual segregation in the South." The new Albright home, built in 1944, was purchased for $8500 with a

20-year mortgage, and was paid off in 1970. There was a celebration when this achievement was met. The home was part of a neighborhood of approximately 125 single-family dwellings located on eight streets that were bordered on the west by apartments on Central Avenue, a project development on the east called Hacienda Village, Will Rogers Memorial Park on the north, and another similar neighborhood on the south. Most of the occupants in the neighborhood were from the South, with many from Texas and Louisiana. In fact, the neighbors next door to us, and those across the street, were from Mom's birth state of Louisiana and hailed from the cities of New Orleans, Monroe, Lake Charles, and Lafayette. All of them and most of the other neighbors moved to Los Angeles in the 1940s for the same reasons as Mom and Dad. Coming from the South and having acquired the behaviors of being honest, hard-working, ethical, prideful, and disciplined, houses were periodically painted, cars were regularly washed by hand, lawns were manicured and trimmed, and flowers were seasonally planted. Most households knew each other as the children attended the same schools, families worshipped at one of several churches in the area, kids could not play or visit each other without the parents meeting first, and most adults in the neighborhood co-supervised children and would report any misbehavior. They would also feed you if parents were working. The neighborhood was a great "village to raise a child" long before this phrase became popular in the United States in the 1980s and '90s.

During a check-up with Dr. Taylor when I was two, he diagnosed a hydrocele, a fluid-filled sac surrounding a testicle that results in swelling of the area. This required surgery to repair.

While surgery of this nature was fairly routine, the idea that Mom's baby boy had to undergo "the knife" was troubling to her, and was on the heels of not walking until I was sixteen months due to having a Vitamin D deficiency. Dad told the story for years that he turned and looked away as he fed me cod liver oil, which is rich in Vitamin D. According to him, I licked the spoon every time he gave me a dose of the medicine he couldn't stand. I guess my body knew what it needed.

Mother Dear was visiting the Albright family from Philadelphia at the time to see her newest grandchild. She accompanied Mom and me to the hospital on the day of the surgery to remove the hydrocele. Dad remained home, as he hated hospitals, and couldn't fathom the idea that his son was undergoing surgery, particularly on the part of the body where it would occur. As I came out from under the anesthesia, Mom said that the first faint words out of my mouth were "Mother Dear?" Mom humorously told this story for years, and declared that while she was happy about my connection with my grandmother, she was shocked, as she was the one who carried me for nine months and brought me into the world. It was she I should have called for first.

Mom and Dad wanted to have other children to increase the Albright clan, and to this end, Alfred Charles was born 20 February 1951, but succumbed to a brain tumor after living six hours. He was named after two of Dad's closest friends working with him at the post office: Alfred Thomas, who was my godfather (and his wife Ruth Thomas was my second godmother); and Charles McWhorter. Again they attempted to expand the family, but Mom's next pregnancy resulted in a miscarriage. She was now in her mid-30s, and the difficulty she had over the years to bear children led her and Dad to conclude that I would grow up an only child.

Initially, this was acceptable to me, except that I noticed that all of my friends in the neighborhood had brothers and sisters, and this reality led me to start praying for a baby brother. I was six when this nightly ritual began and I always ended the prayer by making this wish. Dad told me years later that he and Mom decided to try again in hopes I wouldn't wear out my knee-caps. My prayers were eventually answered, because two days before Mom turned forty, Dr. Taylor assisted her in giving birth to Gerald Anthony Albright on 30 August 1957. He weighed 9 pounds 3 ounces. His name broke the tradition of naming chil-dren after other relatives or close friends. Charles McWhorter and his wife Mamie became Gerald's godparents, along with Leanna Stafford, who lived next door to us on 104th Street. I was ecstatic at having a baby brother, and vowed to be his protector. I even endured the occasional urination in my face while help-ing Mom give him baths. The family was complete in terms of numbers, though a couple of years later, when I was ten, I asked Mom if she could take Gerald back because he was always get-ting into my belongings.

Family life was very traditional in the Albright household during the 1950s and '60s. Dad was the primary breadwinner and Mom was the homemaker, though she held some part-time positions at a cleaners and Sawaya's Department Store to help make ends meet and keep some money in her wallet. She was an excellent cook, like many African-American women from the South, and most meals during the week were made from scratch and included meat or fish, a starch food of some sort, and always a vegetable. A homemade pie, cobbler, or cake rounded out most dinners. The family routinely ate together, and when the call to dinner was made by Mom, whether Gerald and I were in the house or outside, you had no more than ten minutes to wash up and be seated at the table, or there would be consequences. You also had to eat what was prepared, as Mom refused to be a short-order cook. All food on the plate had to be consumed, with Mom and Dad periodically reminding us to "remember all of the less-fortunate children in the world who may have little or nothing to eat." They were transmitting to us the values by which they had been raised.

The dining room and kitchen tables were the centers of family life in the household. Everything from eating, playing games, doing homework, to entertaining visitors and learning the ways of life occurred at these pieces of furniture in our home. I wrote the following poem in 1992 to capture the importance of the table to the Albrights and many other families in the day:

THE TABLE

The table is so important in life
From the moment of one's first breath
The table is there through ups and downs
And remains there until your death

Many hours are spent at this center of life
The tales are embedded in its grain
It records the annals of all family life
And embodies the pleasure and pain

At the table countless meals are consumed
By all who reside within
At the table sit those with abounding love
On whom you could always depend

The table is where discussion ensues
On events and problems at hand
The table is where the heads of the home
Design the family plan

The table is where visitors convene
To share their thoughts of the day
The table is where sad news is aired
That a loved one has passed away

The table is where scoldings are given
About duties that have been shirked
At the table numerous hours are spent
Performing the daily schoolwork

Family Life

The table is where most ethics are honed
By separating wrong from right
At the table the basic tools to survive
Are fed both day and night

The table is truly a wonderful place
Though not valued till time passes by
When recalling the factors that influence life
The table soars high in the sky

The table has etched deep in its soul
The history of lives to a stage
And though one table is left behind
A new table turns the page

For to pass the tradition that guides a life
Is a duty as one grows old
All must listen to the tales of the table
The history of life will be told

Of course, as children grow up they tend to seek their independence and challenge the parental rule of law, and Gerald and I were no exception. While there were a number of tests on my part, the one I remember the most was when I was seven and mom needed something from the neighborhood Rexall Drugstore on Central Avenue. Like most local stores, workers in these establishments were an extension of the family, and you came to know them from frequent patronage. Such was the case at this drugstore, as Mom became close with a particular saleswoman. While they were conversing, I was patrolling the store aisles and came upon the section where stationery supplies resided. A pencil with a tassel on the end and a large two-inch eraser caught my eye, and for some unknown reason, I decided that I needed to "procure" these objects, totaling about fifteen cents for both. After looking around the store, I placed them in my pocket without taking them to the counter to see if Mom would pay for them. When we arrived home, I removed the items from my pocket and placed them in the kitchen drawer where all other stationery supplies were housed—"a place for everything and everything in its place." I learned that day that Mom was not only going to meet my challenge, but also was the consummate homemaker and knew everything about the household. Later that afternoon, my full name, "William Dudley Albright, Jr." was called out and the following question trailed: "Where did this pencil and eraser come from?" I sheepishly replied, as I had no other response, "I stole them." Mom came to the room where I was doing whatever, grabbed me by my ear, threw me in the car, and took me back to the local drugstore. With my head bowed and tail tucked, Mom declared out loud to all within listening distance, which meant everyone in the store, that "this big-head boy stole these items from this store and I want all to know it."

"Mattie Pearl," said the saleswoman, "that's okay, let him have them. I will cover the costs."

Mom responded, "Oh no, I am breaking this shit up right now."

Mom and I returned home and she marched me into her bedroom where Dad was sleeping to inform him of what I had done. The combination of the total embarrassment in the drugstore and the subsequent belt-whipping I received from my father left an indelible mark on my understanding of what's right and wrong. That was the last time I procured something that didn't belong to me, or wasn't paid for, though there were other lessons to be learned. Clearly, that "shit" was broken up.

Gerald also decided to challenge the parental code on a number of occasions because he was mischievous, but not uncontrollable. For example, 103rd street ran east and west, and was the primary thoroughfare that split the Watts community in half from north to south. Most of the major businesses in Watts resided on this motorway, including the cleaners and Sawaya's Department Store where Mom worked. Many of these businesses as well as some homes were burned during the riots of August 1965. One evening during the riots, I was awakened by the sound of water hitting the roof, and thought that the fires would be extinguished by the rain. I peeked outside my bedroom window and saw no rain. After running outside to see what was happening, I saw Dad on our tar-shingled roof watering it down with the hose. I asked him why he was doing that, and he told me to look to the west.

When I did, I saw a wall of fire, contrasted against the darkness of the midnight sky, which was produced by the torching of Shop-Rite Super Market on Central Avenue. The market was exploding from the fire and launching projectiles that were causing fires on business and housing structures nearby. Dad was attempting to minimize the damage to our home by wetting the roof. He succeeded, as no damage occurred to our home or any close-by neighbors. 103rd was also a border street for Will Rogers Park, and consequently served as the northern boundary for the neighborhood where we lived.

Unlike 104th that was a residential street that had little traffic, 103rd was a busy thoroughfare. At the age of three, Gerald, or Jerry as Mom called him, was warned not to ride his tricycle on 103rd, and to stay on 104th where he was safe and known. After calling for him several times, Mom suspected that he had ignored her admonishment and was riding on 103rd. In the event that she was right, she decided to visit the peach tree in the backyard that produced not only luscious peaches for eating and canning, but effective switches that could be used when a child disobeyed. Upon leaving the house looking for him, she decided to walk east on 104th Street, which bent to the north towards 103rd, knowing that the last time she saw Jerry he was traveling west. As she reached 103rd she looked west and saw Jerry leisurely pedaling east on the same street. She was correct—he had disobeyed her orders. She was about 30 yards away from and walking toward him when he looked up, saw her, performed a 180-degree move that took much longer than he wanted, and attempted to speed away. He was too slow—Mom was on him, and his three-year-old legs could not pedal fast enough to escape her and the peach tree switch that tapped his calves. This tapping lasted all the way home and then some after they went inside. As a child, it was the last time Jerry ventured onto 103rd Street by himself without receiving permission.

As there were three males in the household, Dad also had his occasions to observe Mom's determination, though one instance, in particular, took on a totally different character. As a result of being the primary breadwinner for the family, working one full-time job at the post office where he took on increasing responsibilities, one part-time job for a number of years at the automobile club, and then some odd jobs like painting and hauling to supplement his income, Dad developed duodenal ulcers, an illness that can range from being shallow in nature to deep and life-threatening. He had had a couple of attacks over the years, but on this one occasion after midnight, and while having the urge to have a bowel movement, he voided nothing but blood and eventually passed out. While transitioning into an unconscious state, he called for Mom with a much-weakened voice. She responded by going to the bathroom and slapping him in an attempt to keep him conscious. She continued to do so while calling the emergency personnel using the old rotary-style telephone that fortunately was right outside the bathroom door sitting on a hall table. When they arrived, they found Dad back in the bed, with Mom continuing to slap him and administering whatever additional aid she thought would be beneficial. It worked, and though Dad remained in a life-threatening state, she had done much to give him a chance to live.

He did live for many years afterwards, but following his rehabilitation from this near-death experience, he inquired of Mom how he ended up back in bed prior to the emergency personnel arriving. Mom smiled, raised her right eyebrow—which she could do effectively when she wanted to communicate a point with emphasis—and informed him that she had accomplished that feat. After his recuperation, he shared with me that Mom had an inner strength and determination that are uncommon, and that he had an elevated level of love and respect for her. With Mom's cooking and overall tender loving care, dad overcame the ulcers as well as a subsequent bout of colon cancer in 1979. They shared sixty years of marriage until September 8, 2003 when he passed away.

As Mom was always there nurturing and serving as the backbone to the family, she seldom missed significant events of family members, regardless of whether or not travel was involved, or the status of her health. She attended the commencement ceremonies for my undergraduate and graduate degrees, my 50th birthday celebration in Nassau, Bahamas while in a wheelchair, and the weddings of my two daughters including one in Ocho Rios, Jamaica and the other in Los Angeles, again being wheelchair-bound. Likewise for Gerald, she was in attendance at the Grammys when he received his first nomination, and missed his graduation from college only due to Dad's recovery from colon cancer surgery in 1979. If it had not been for failing health, she would have attended the Grammys for Gerald's additional nominations and when he received other significant honors. Even though she passed in 2006, I am sure her spirit was in the audience when I received the Black Engineer of the Year for Diversity Leadership in 2010 and the GEM Consortium's Employer of the Year and Lifetime Achievement Awards in 2011.

One of the methods used by Mom and Dad to shape the morals, values and ethics of Gerald and myself was regular attendance at church. Both of them belonged to Baptist churches, Mom a member of Antioch Baptist Church in Shreveport, and Dad a member of Mt. Olive Baptist Church in Frankston, TX. Neither of them was overly religious, but rather had more of a spiritual orientation in their beliefs and faith. They were guided more by the teachings of the New Testament in the Bible than they were the Old Testament, and conveyed to Gerald and me that whatever relationship we had with God was to be determined by us individually. However, they also believed that regular attendance at church would help us distinguish right from wrong, develop our abilities to effectively interact with others, grow our leadership skills through participation in various church organizations, and give us a venue to learn how to speak or play an instrument in front of an audience.

Shortly after we settled in the Watts community in 1950, the Albrights started attending Beulah Baptist Church. It was located on the corner of Success Avenue and 100th Street and was within walking distance from our home. Dad and I walked each Sunday to attend Sunday School, and Mom appeared with Gerald after he was born, in time to attend the regular service that began at eleven o'clock. The church's pastor, Reverend Jodie O. Barnett, hailed from the Cherokee and Anderson Counties of East Texas, and the Barnett and Albright families knew each other. As she did at Antioch in Shreveport, Mom sang in the choir, was a member of the Missionary Society, served as secretary of the church for many years, and led a number of programs to raise money for the church. Dad was an active member of the Trustee Board, taught

Sunday School, and was instrumental in saving the church from being torn down when the city desired to extend 100th Street. He also took care of the church's grounds, mowed the grass weekly, and planted flowers yearly. I was a member of the Junior Usher Board, became a Junior Deacon, and sang in the Junior Choir. Gerald was young during most of this activity, but by the age of ten was clearly developing his piano and saxophone skills, and played at the church on special occasions.

By the mid-1950s, the membership of Beulah had grown to the size where Mom and Dad thought that a credit union would be ideal. As not-for-profit institutions, credit unions are structured to serve their members rather than to maximize profits, and as such, they encourage thrift among the membership through regular savings and the provision of loans to members at favorable interest rates. Mom and Dad concluded that establishing a credit union under the umbrella of a church like Beulah—with a membership of around five hundred adults at the time—could not fail with the right type of leadership and management. Following the receipt of great enthusiasm on the part of the church's membership, Mom drafted the proposed by-laws that would be used to operate the credit union, and secured the agreement of a number of members who not only agreed to join the credit union, but serve on the board as well.

She completed the application, and submitted it and the proposed by-laws to the National Credit Union Association (NCUA). The NCUA approved the application, and in 1958, the Beulah Baptist Church Federal Credit Union (BBFCU) became a reality, with Mom as its Managing Treasurer, and Dad a member of the Board. Mom served in her credit union capacity while also serving as the secretary to the church until 1974. She had an office at the church where she performed her secretarial responsibilities, and converted part of the den at our home into an office where she executed her credit union role. Monthly credit union board meetings were held at the house with refreshments that Mom prepared, and the annual shareholders' meeting was held at the church. The annual meetings were always structured to make them interesting and informative to secure high attendance on the part of credit union members. In addition to the normal business agenda that included determining that a quorum was present, approval of the minutes of the last meeting, reports from the president of the board and the managing treasurer, any unfinished and new business, and election of officers and board members, there was always a guest speaker such as a community leader like a councilperson, a representative from the credit union league, or the managing treasurer or president from a neighboring credit union to speak on what was happening in the community, or outlining developments in the credit union movement. After the meeting adjourned, refreshments were always served to allow members and guests to network. When Mom relocated to Texas in 1974, I became the managing treasurer of the credit union and performed that role for one year before I moved to the Washington, DC area in 1975. She passed on a wealth of information and guidance that helped me tremendously during that year.

Concurrent with running the BBFCU, Mom also managed another credit union in Compton, CA for a couple of years to help bring it out of the "red." She regularly attended regional retreats and meetings sponsored by the Credit Union National Association (CUNA) that were usually held at Knott's Berry Farm in Buena Park, CA. Mom was well-respected among her credit union colleagues, as well as by the examiners from the NCUA who conducted annual audits of the books for the two credit unions she managed.

Finally, to enrich her credit union experience, Mom applied for and was granted admission to a three-year executive education program in 1967 that was jointly sponsored by the CUNA and the University of California at Los Angeles (UCLA). In 1969, Mom completed this certificate program with distinction. She attended UCLA for several weeks during the summer months of this three-year period and lived on campus. This left Dad, Gerald, and me to fend for ourselves and take care of the household. By this time Dad had become a supervisor at the post office and had to wear a white dress shirt and tie to work every day. And so in addition to keeping the house clean, and assisting Dad with preparing meals and his lunch which he took to work in a metal lunch pail, I became fairly proficient at washing and ironing dress shirts and other articles of clothing. Sewing on buttons also became part of the process. Mom had prepared us well for her absences from home during this three-year period, and some of the clothes-washing and repair expertise that was evident within the Dabner family over the years was being continued by me, though not professionally.

Probably one of the most meaningful family events occurred in July 1993 when Mom and Dad celebrated their 50th year of marriage in Berryville, TX where they were living at the time.

Celebrating birthdays and anniversaries was extremely important to the Albrights, and it is for this reason that Gerald and I and our respective families sponsored the observance of this important milestone. Mom was deeply involved in the planning of the event, and rather than observe it in their anniversary month of September, she chose the July 4 weekend of that year, allowing as many family members as possible to attend. This weekend also coincided with the reunion of the Lyle Family being held in Shreveport, and consequently, Dennie Lyle Dabner, Clifton (Mom's brother), and many of their children, grandchildren, and other relatives drove 100 miles from Shreveport to join in on the festivities. All of Mom's grandchildren at the time except one were in attendance and participated in the ceremony. Many neighbors, colleagues, and friends from Berryville and Frankston, including members of the city council and the chamber of commerce, were invited and indeed attended. During the ceremony, Gerald's daughter, Selina, sang the Lord's Prayer at the age of twelve, his son Brandon served as the ring bearer, Mom and Dad renewed their vows, and Dad presented his wife of fifty years with a wedding ring he selected from a jewelry store in Tyler, TX. No longer did she have to wear the ring she bought at the pawn shop fifty years earlier. This newest ring was given to Selina following Mom's passing. Dad also wore a tuxedo for the occasion, only the second time he sported one—the first occurring at the Grammys in 1988. He refused to wear a "monkey suit," as he called tuxedos, except on these two occasions. The ceremony was followed by a reception during which Gerald played his rendition of Luther Vandross' hit song "Here and Now," which was requested of him by Mom. I complemented his performance with two poems, "So Secure" and "A Natural Love," which I had written for the occasion to share with the audience of approximately 150 who sat under a beautiful tent in the front yard of the home on Bright Acres. This is the name the family unofficially labeled our property in Berryville, TX. I presented them with the first copy of a book of poems I published in 1993 entitled "Out of Anger with Love" that contained the two poems I read, as well as a large framed version of the "A Natural Love" poem that incorporated pictures of both of them at the time they were married. Happy tears were shed by many, with most coming from Mom. It was a memorable event, one that many in attendance remember to this day.

During the week of the anniversary celebration, Mom prepared dinner for several of the evenings the family was in town. On one particular evening, Mom prepared one of my favorite meals which included pork neck bones, black-eyed peas and rice, cabbage, and cornbread. As usual, the meal consisted of a meat, a starch, a vegetable, and some bread. Dad jokingly commented that he was happy the family was in town because he was tired of eating leftovers, which generated a glare from Mom analogous to "if looks could kill." After we finished eating, Dad leaned back fully contented after cleaning his plate and remarked, "Mattie Pearl, you got lucky again." Another glare emanated from Mom's eyes. I asked Dad how he determined that Mom was lucky after eating her cooking for fifty years, to which he responded, "I don't want her to become complacent with her cooking—she is almost perfect."

To this statement, Mom blurted out, "Kiss my ass, Dub." "Dub" was the nickname for dad that he had since childhood. We all laughed for several minutes, and then ate some peach cobbler Mom had prepared. Love is truly grand.

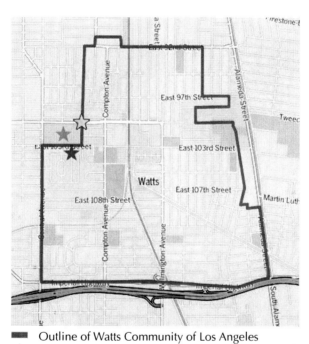

■ Outline of Watts Community of Los Angeles

★ The Albright home at 1329 E. 104th St. in Watts

★ Will Rogers Memorial Park, currently known as
Ted Watkins Memorial Park

☆ Beulah Baptist Church

Mom on the Front Porch of 1329 E. 104th Street,
Los Angeles, CA—June 1961

William D. Albright Jr. at One Month with Mom

Gerald A. Albright at Four Months with Mom—1957

Mom with Sons Bill and Gerald in Los Angeles with Gerald's Godmother, Leanna Stafford, in the background—August 1959

Beulah Baptist Church Where the Albrights Worshipped and That Sponsored the Federal Credit Union

Class Picture of CUNA/UCLA Executive Management Program—1969

CUNA District Four School
for
Credit Union Personnel

Certificate of Completion

This is to certify that

Mattie P. Albright

has satisfactorily completed the course of instruction in Credit Union Executive Training. This course was jointly sponsored by the leagues of the Fourth District Credit Union National Association, and the University of California, Los Angeles.

Course completed on August 15, 1969.

Chairman of Local Administrative Committee

University Coordinator

Director of School

The Albrights — 1974

Mom, Gerald, and his wife Glynis at The Grammys in 1988

Mom and Dad in Philadelphia Visiting Family—1989

The Extended Dabner Family, Including Mom and Her Brothers George Jr., Clifton and Wife Susie (Dennie) Standing in the Center—1989

Mom and Dad Celebrating Their 50th Anniversary and Renewing Their Vows with Rev. Mellie Arps Officiating—Berryville, TX; July 1993

A NATURAL LOVE

Sometimes we watch with wonder
At the twinkling of the stars and birds in flight
Then there is the moon that appears
And the sun rising each morning and setting each night

We think of how perfect the natural world is
With its balance and all things fitting together
There is also the quest for the perfect love
One like nature that will live forever

And we look and smile at each other
Realizing that we have the ideal love
A love so real and deep and warm
Just as natural as the stars above

A natural love is like the flower that blooms each spring
So dependable and filled with beauty and life
A natural love is like an old oak tree
With deep roots like those created by husband and wife

A natural love is like the river that is fed by streams
It grows each and every day
A natural love is like a raging fire
Where passion is hot like an August day

From dawn till the sun sets and we close our eyes
We are in each other's thoughts throughout the day
We dream of one another while sleeping at night
With these constant thoughts we will not go astray

We are natural, our love is pure
Like snowflakes falling gently to earth
Our love is exciting and filled with glorious wonder
Like a newborn baby on the day of its birth

Our love is special and is never-ending
Our love is a perfect fit like a hand in glove
Together we are one and incomplete when apart
Like a perfect nature, ours is a natural love

A natural love is like the deep blue sea
Though calm one day a storm it can bring
A natural love is like the sounds of spring
When rivers are flowing and robins sing

A natural love is all-consuming
And we inhale each other with every breath
A natural love is a once in a lifetime union
And we will love each other completely until our death

Copyright © 1991 by William D. Albright

SO SECURE

I awoke this morning and reached out for you
Touching you made me feel safe and warm
You reached out and firmly held my hand
I knew I was protected from any harm

My eyes cleared up and focused on you
What a beautiful sight it was to see
You gently gave me a morning kiss
My life was filled with love and security

And as we departed to our daily tasks
I felt so secure, complete, and alive
You are my comfort and tower of strength
And I depend on the truth and confidence in your eyes

I feel so secure with you in my life
Like a bird in its nest, it feels no harm
I feel so secure with you in my life
Like a baby wrapped in its mother's arms

I feel so secure with you in my life
Like money that is guarded in the bank
I feel so secure with you in my life
I love you deeply and I have God to thank

After a hard day's work I return to our nest
To talk with you and feel revived
Whatever problems I had during the day
Vanished quickly upon seeing your eyes

Life is so wonderful being with you
I can't imagine living it alone
I lived in a house before we met
Now with you it has become a home

And now that I'm ready to close my eyes
At the slow disappearance of day's light
It's comforting to know as I lay my head
You're the first I see at dawn and the last I see at night

I feel so secure with you in my life
Like a bird in its nest, it feels no harm
I feel so secure with you in my life
Like a baby wrapped in its mother's arms

I feel so secure with you in my life
Like money that is guarded in the bank
I feel so secure with you in my life
I love you deeply and I have God to thank

The annual road trips the Albright family took were adventurous and exciting. Mom and Dad would plan the trips with assistance from the Automobile Club of America (AAA), including the scenic stops on the way to our final destination, usually to see one side of the family or the other. This meant traveling to Texas, Louisiana, or Pennsylvania. AAA always prepared TripTiks for our journey and I learned at an early age how to read and follow them. In the 1950s and early '60s, and as African-Americans, the family always drove through the Jim Crow South, since we couldn't afford airfare, and more importantly, it was usually safer to be riding in your own automobile. This was preferable to depending upon taxis, public transportation, hotels/motels, etc., as you never knew what you would encounter in terms of ill-treatment due to race. Even when you were driving in the South, racial trouble could confront the family.

During one such trip in 1960, when we were driving to Philadelphia, PA to see Mom's side of the family, Dad decided to get an oil change and lube job in Birmingham, Alabama on the new Plymouth Belvedere purchased earlier in the year. We pulled into a gas station during a rainstorm and received some interesting looks from white patrons of the establishment, probably due to our blackness and our California tags. Dad approached the owner and made his request for the needed services. The owner agreed and had one of his technicians drive the car on the rack. Meanwhile, Mom had three-year-old Gerald in her arms and me by the hand as we ran through the rain toward the restroom. It was locked. Upon returning to the station office, Mom informed the owner of the locked facility to which he responded, "We don't have no colored bathroom."

Of course by now the car was on the rack and empty of oil. The family remained quiet and positioned under the overhang of the roofline so as to avoid being soaked by the downpour. Following the completion of the service on the car, the rack was lowered and the technician removed the car from the garage. Dad paid the tab. As the family loaded up the car to drive off, the owner approached Dad and inquired if he was interested in purchasing gas. He refused. It was clear that the color of his money was acceptable, but that the color of our skin was not acceptable enough to use the toilet.

Unless there was an emergency, we usually took a circuitous route to some fascinating points of interest before arriving at our final destination. The Grand Canyon, Painted Desert, Royal Gorge, Petrified Forest, Pueblo of Sandia Village, New York, Washington DC, and some of the national parks were destinations visited. Mom and Dad enjoyed seeing America, as they had planned a few months before I was born, and now they wanted to share these adventures with me and later Gerald. In addition to packing all necessary clothes needed for the trip, Mom would prepare and pack some food, which usually included fried chicken and fruit that could be consumed while we were on the road, as well as eggs and bacon to be prepared on our portable Coleman white gas stove and eaten at a road-side park. Juices, water, and other items were kept on ice in a red aluminum Coca-Cola cooler. In the 1950s, ice used while traveling came in a big block that could be purchased from an ice machine usually at filling (gas) stations. There were no bags of ice cubes at that time. Dad always packed an ice pick to break up the ice block so it would fit in the cooler.

We typically departed Los Angeles at night around eleven o'clock or midnight so that we would be driving through the Mojave Desert in the early morning when it was the coolest, and even then it was in the high nineties during the summer. Dad usually hung a large canvas bag of water over the hood ornament of the car, and kept an appropriate roll of tape in the trunk in the event the water hose to the radiator ruptured while driving in the desert, a common occurrence. There were no computer games and DVDs to occupy our time, so while we were on the road, Gerald and I either slept, counted the number of cars on freight trains, pleaded for the conductor to blow the train's whistle, or attempted to see how many states we could identify by viewing the license plates of cars we passed or that passed us. And there was always an empty Folgers coffee can so that Mom could help Gerald and me void our liquid waste when we were very young. Dad stopped only to gas up, have the oil changed and car lubed, to see something of interest, or to purchase some food.

During one road trip to Texas to see my paternal grandparents when I was seven, Dad regaled me with the importance of his birthplace, Frankston, TX. He prepped me with much informa-tion about the Lone Star State, including the broadly touted perception that "everything is big in Texas." As we approached the city limits, Mom and Dad woke me from my sleep in the backseat to prepare to see my grandmother. As my eyes cleared and became focused we were just passing the city sign for Frankston that advertised a population of 1200 individuals. I was living in the city of Los Angeles which boasted a population of millions, and seeing the Frankston sign immediately put me in a hysterical state of laughter that lasted for a couple of hours, a feat kids could achieve at my age at the time. Once we arrived at Grandmother Mozell's home, he laughingly told her and others that I "hurt his feelings about his hometown."

In addition to providing great family time, these road trips significantly influenced my understanding of the United States, and enhanced my appreciation of just how beautiful the country is by the viewing it from the ground. Driving became part of my blood, and I developed the habit of motoring to various destinations in the country after I was grown. This resulted in several cross-country trips from coast to coast, as well as road trips to Texas to see the folks.

One such trip occurred in 2005 to spend Thanksgiving with Mom. Dad had passed away two years earlier, and the family thought that driving down to spend this family-oriented holiday with Mom would be fun and meaningful. She was eighty-six at this point, with declining health, and to make everything easier on all involved, my wife Lydia decided to purchase most of the food for the Thanksgiving dinner in advance and take it with us to Texas. To this end, we had the turkey prepared and cooked at the company where my wife worked, purchased a number of the side dishes from QVC, and went to the grocery store to obtain the remaining items for the meal. Given the amount and type of food we had to take to Texas and the number of passengers traveling, I rented a recreational vehicle (RV) large enough to accommodate four adults, two children, and a dog. The RV came equipped with a refrigerator to protect the food. We also needed the additional sleeping quarters the RV provided once we arrived at Mom's home, as it was too small to comfortably sleep all of us. Given the cold temperatures that were prevalent in late November 2005, it was recommended by the owner of the RV company to winterize the vehicle, which meant that the bathroom and sink could not be utilized, as the pipes were filled with anti-freeze instead of water. This would require us to make periodic stops while on the road.

And so on the Tuesday morning before Thanksgiving in 2005, Lydia and I, one daughter, Denee, her four-year-old daughter, Mika, six-month-old son Mateo, and Canaan the dog, set out driving 1200 miles to Frankston in East Texas in a colorful RV with "RENT ME" posted in large letters on both sides of the cab along with a picture of a man wearing a cowboy hat. My son-in-law, Eugene, planned to fly to Tyler, Texas, which he did, and join us on the return road trip home. I drove the entire trip. Canaan was a six-year-old Boston Terrier that had undergone a surgical procedure performed on his left hind leg, and as such, had to wear a cone around his head to prevent him from gnawing at his bandages. Canaan was extremely close to me and at every stop along the way, if Lydia vacated the front passenger seat, he would assume the position of serving as the navigator for the trip. He was a great companion during the 2400-mile round trip.

The family thought we were the "Black Griswolds," referring to National Lampoon's movie *Vacation* starring Chevy Chase, in which he took the Griswold family on vacation to "Wally World." Instead of the family riding in a station wagon, we were a five-member black family riding in a "RENT ME" RV traveling down south with a cone-head Boston Terrier. While we were clearly not the first African-American family to drive a reasonably large RV through the South, we were clearly a unique sight to many who passed us or whom we passed on the interstate, given the number of double takes we experienced.

The plan was to reach Birmingham, Alabama by the evening of the first day, and reach Mom's home by the afternoon of the next day (Wednesday). The plan was implemented to perfection, even though we had to make frequent stops given the makeup of the travelers. By Tuesday evening, I was pulling into the parking lot of a motel on the outskirts of Birmingham. The marquee of the motel said nothing about being dog-friendly, so Lydia went to the front desk to secure two rooms, while I walked Canaan to do his business. I then entered the back door of the motel with Canaan in my arms, crept up the back stairs, and entered our room. All was well. The next morning, I walked Canaan again, placed him in the RV, and went to the front desk to pay our bill. While standing at the counter, I glanced up and observed a bank of television monitors that showed all entrances to the motel as well as the stairways including the one I traversed while "sneaking" Canaan into the room. I called Lydia up to the counter, showed her the monitors, and we both fell out laughing thinking how foolish I must have looked to any observers of my attempt to get Canaan into the motel without detection.

We continued our laughter as we observed several other patrons walking their canines through the motel. We joined the remainder of the family in the dining area, consumed some quick breakfast, and resumed our junket toward East Texas.

By Wednesday afternoon, Thanksgiving Eve, we arrived at Mom's home on Bright Acres, plugged the camper into an electrical outlet in the garage, and began a wonderful three-day visit with her and her live-in caretaker. Of course we regaled them with our experiences driving the RV to Texas. Mom was able to meet Mika and Mateo, two of her great-grandchildren, for the first time, as well as Canaan, whom she wanted to keep since she loved dogs. Thanksgiving dinner was delightful and delicious, and our decision to bring the meal was a great one as we only had to heat up the food, enjoy each other's company at the table, and take care of the minimal amount of cleanup. We departed Bright Acres the following Saturday for our day and a half road trip home with one extra passenger, my son-in-law. We arrived as planned on Sunday evening. The trip was a total success, and it was the last time Mom celebrated Thanksgiving. It was also the last time I saw her alive. She passed away 18 March 2006.

Chapter 7
Mattie Leaves Los Angeles with Reluctance and Relocates to East Texas

During the late 1960s, Dad was contacted by his mother, Mozell Cantley Campbell, to tell him that her sisters and brothers were thinking of selling their property in Frankston off Route 175 that they inherited from their father, John Cantley. The last name Campbell came from her second husband following a divorce from Dad's father, George Albright. Grandmother Mozell was born September 25, 1898 in Frankston, and lived most of her life in the city with the exception of a few years when she lived in Wichita Falls, TX. She had three sisters, one brother, and one half-brother, all born in Frankston, and only one of these siblings had a child to whom property could be bequeathed. All of my grandmother's siblings had moved either to other cities in Texas or out of state: Ernest to Jacksonville, TX; Nina to Wichita Falls, TX; Mable and Elga to Los Angeles; and Ethel to Denver, CO. Upon receiving the information about their respective tracts of land, Dad called each of them to request that they let him know first if they were indeed going to sell their land that summed up to a total of about 120 acres. At first blush, they all thought he wasn't serious, and wouldn't leave the big city of Los Angeles to return to his roots in rural East Texas. He convinced them otherwise—that it was important to keep as much of the original Cantley land intact for future generations, especially since he had two sons. Dad was a firm believer that it was necessary to have sons when land was involved, and in this case, to keep the property as "Albright Land." He feared that having daughters, who would someday get married, would be subject to the whims and decisions of their husbands, thereby possibly jeopardizing the status of the land. Having the land would also give him another option to consider upon retirement from the post office. Over the next couple of years, Dad did purchase the land from his aunts and uncles, realizing that he would inherit his mother's part of the Cantley legacy and that of his father, George Albright, who had acreage in Henderson County approximately five miles from the Cantley property. George Albright, known as Papa, was born 1 March 1893 and died 22 June 1958. He had been a sharecropper for years, but eventually put himself in a position to purchase the 100-acre tract of land outright from its previous owner, John L. Stone, in February 1925.

Following his near-death experiences caused by severe duodenal ulcers and his successful rehabilitation, Dad became convinced that he needed to leave the asphalt jungle of Los Angeles and live in quieter surroundings if he was going to enjoy his golden years. The increased traffic and crime in the city, changes occurring within the postal service, and stresses brought on by wondering how Gerald's college education was going to be financed, among other things, had taken a toll on him and he felt it wasn't going to improve in the short run. I had graduated from the University of Redlands in 1971 with a BS degree in chemistry, and my student loans and finances

toward any graduate education were going to be my responsibility. In 1971, Gerald was still in junior high school and so
the issue of paying for his college education was a real one. In
Dad's mind, the gamble of purchasing the land coupled with
the property he would eventually inherit would give him the
opportunity to return to the farm, raise some cattle, eat fresh
food, and breathe fresh air. Los Angeles was notorious for its
smog in the '60s, '70s, and '80s, as more and more residents
owned cars. In 1973, Dad approached Mom with his proposal
and rationale to relocate to Frankston over the following year.
By 1974, he would have worked at the post office for twenty-
eight years, and this coupled with the three years in the Army
would give him more than thirty years in support of the federal
government. This achievement would provide him with additional benefits in retirement. The idea of moving to Frankston
was not received warmly at all by Mom, and in fact, introduced
some significant strife in the family for some time that had not
been seen before by Gerald and me. Many discussions and ar-
guments occurred, inclusive of four-letter words. Mom clearly
understood the dilemma. She empathized with Dad's concern
about his health, having helped him survive on more than one
occasion. But she was raised in Shreveport, a reasonably large
city that offered many cultural activities, fashion, and family life
even though she was subject to the Jim Crow South of the '20s,
'30s, and '40s. This lifestyle was then elevated by the experiences she had in Los Angeles, and she had a comfortable home
that was paid for, many friends and activities in which she was
engaged, and moreover, two sons she would be leaving behind.
She would be sacrificing this to move to rural East Texas where
she had no friends, knew only her mother-in-law with whom

there existed a cool relationship, and only a few acquaintances established as a result of traveling almost yearly to this area to see Dad's mother and other members of his family. There were a couple of friends with whom she went to school at CC High, still living in Shreveport, but they were 100 miles away—not exactly what you call neighbors. A number of her Shreveport friends moved to Los Angeles as she did in the 1940s, and she would be leaving them behind in "La La Land."

The family convened a meeting in early 1974 to discuss Dad's proposed move to Texas for him and Mom. It was clear that the two of them had given much thought to how best to make this work, discussing the pros and cons of various alternatives. The one option that floated to the top and appeared to be the best was for me to move back home, take care of the house in Watts, and oversee Gerald for his last year in high school. He would be going to college somewhere. I was twenty-four at the time, working at The Aerospace Corporation as a senior personnel representative, and was pursuing my Masters in Business Administration from the California State University at Dominguez Hills. I had graduated from David Starr Jordan High School in Watts, moved from home in 1971 shortly after graduating from the University of Redlands, and was living in an apartment with a roommate, Russell Flye. Dad's proposal included having Russell move into the house with me, as there were enough bedrooms to accommodate Gerald, Russell, and me, and that plan would place two adults in the house to manage the property, and Gerald. Since the house was paid for, we would also be saving rent money, and needed to pay only for utilities and other general expenses. I was deeply trusted by my parents and seen as a responsible son, a character shaped in part by that embarrassing moment in the drugstore when I was seven years old, and the subsequent whipping I received. The plan presented was acceptable to me, and as the family discussion continued, Mom appeared to feel increasingly comfortable with the move as far as the well-being of her sons was concerned. She remained very much dissatisfied with leaving Los Angeles in general and wondered how her life would be affected and how she would spend her time in Frankston. She realized, however, that if things did not work out, she had a home in Los Angeles and her two sons to move back to—a backup plan that most individuals in this type of situation didn't have. Like Mother Dear, she was independent, resourceful, and determined. She would survive. Dad was delighted as Mom stood by his side, a vow she took for better or for worse.

And so Mom and Dad relocated to Frankston, Texas in the summer of 1974. She was fifty-seven and he was fifty-eight, and both had lots of energy in the tank. While Mom remained unsure about the move, Dad was overjoyed at leaving Los Angeles, which he thought would present him with a premature death if he remained in the city. He left for Texas before Mom in order to begin getting the house where my grandfather lived in shape to accommodate the two of them on a temporary basis until he could build another house he promised her.

My grandfather, George Albright, lived in a two-bedroom home that was approaching at least eighty years of age when Dad and Mom moved in. It was made of wood, but had a brick fireplace and a tin roof that could easily lull you to sleep when it was hit by raindrops. Instead of sitting on a concrete foundation, the old house stood on two rows of cinder blocks that were positioned at the corners and in the middle to provide support. The front porch and steps did reach the ground. The house did not have many occupants following my grandfather's death in 1958, and that of his second wife, Pearl Albright, who passed in 1969. George and Pearl were married in March 1924 following his divorce from my grandmother Mozell. Dad was seven years old when his father and stepmother were married. In 1974, and at the age of fifty-eight, Dad was quite aware that the old house needed much work to make it livable for him and Mom.

By the end of the summer in 1974, Mom was in Texas helping Dad achieve the goal of fixing up the house. My roommate and I moved back into the house at 1329 East 104th Street, and Gerald began his senior year at Alain Locke High School. One year later in October 1975, however, I relocated to the Washington, DC area to work for the east coast operations of The Aerospace Corporation. As a result of this decision and move on my part, Dad convinced Mom to sell the home in Los Angeles, as they could use the equity for their home in Texas. The house sold for $22,000. Gerald entered college at the University of Redlands, and started living with Leanna Stafford during his college breaks. Leanna was Gerald's godmother who lived next door to 1329. Finally, Mom's safety net disappeared of having a home in Los Angeles if the situation in Frankston didn't work out.

The death of Dad's Mother Mozell in 1977, at the age of seventy-nine, and his bout of colon cancer in 1979 rounded out the first five years for him and Mom in East Texas. Following

Dad's recuperation, they began working on plans for the new home. The decision was made to move Mozell's small home from its position on Route 175 in Frankston to a knoll located about seventy-five yards behind my grandfather's home, which served as their temporary headquarters. Placed on a large foundation, my grandmother's home served as the core for the new home and provided the living and dining rooms, one bedroom, a small bathroom and kitchen. To this were added a master bedroom and bathroom, a family room, central heating and air conditioning, a utility room for a washer, dryer, and two freezers, a two-car garage, and a fenced-in patio. The new home, completed in 1982, was comparable in size to the home in Los Angeles, provided much more comfort than their temporary quarters, and was spacious enough to accommodate some visitors. Some of the original furniture from the Los Angeles home that I took with me when I relocated to the Washington, DC area was transferred to the new home in Frankston/Berryville area to complete the project.

Founded in 1902, Frankston, Texas was named after Miss Frankie Miller, who donated land for the downtown city park that remains to this day. The town was founded when the Texas and New Orleans Railroad was built through the area. The city is nestled in the northeast section of Anderson County where state highways 175 and 155 intersect. For many years, this intersection was controlled by a blinking red light, but was eventually upgraded to a four-way stop light with left-turn arrows due to the widening of the roads and the increase in car and truck traffic. Lumber was the first industry of Frankston, and cotton was the basis of the economy around 1925. The community also relied on other crops such as corn, and various types of peas, peaches, pears, and tomatoes to supplement incomes. Most of the community's businesses were on the town square, but employment opportunities were limited with many residents commuting within 25 miles to the larger cities of Tyler to the north, Palestine to the south, Athens to the west, and Jacksonville to the east to work and shop. This remains true to this day.

According to the 2010 census, Frankston had just over 1200 individuals who resided in the city, with about 80% being listed as white, and 15% black. The median income for a household in the town was slightly below $46,000 and about 7% of the population was below the poverty level.

Berryville, Texas, a smaller version of Frankston in terms of population, but with a white population of 91% and less than 4% black, is named after James E. Berry, who founded the city. The city is located off highway 155 just a few miles north of Frankston, and is in the southeastern corner of Henderson County. The original settlement, on the Neches River, grew up after the Civil War. There were a few stores and churches for the population of about 500, but by the late 1890s, the town began to decline and all commercial activity evaporated. This turned around with the construction of the Blackburn Crossing Dam on the river, which began in 1960 and completed in 1962. There was an enhancement to the dam in the 1969-1972 timeframe, and the City of Berryville was incorporated in 1972. The construction of the dam created Lake Palestine, which has a surface area of over 25,000 acres that has facilitated water conservation, wildlife preservation, and recreation. Fishing and boating became popular activities for citizens living on or near the lake, and it became a draw for retirees and others who built both primary and vacation homes. The population began to expand with the number of inhabitants in Berryville and the overall Lake Palestine area growing to approximately 1000 and 6000 respectively. With this population expansion various businesses began to spring up including motels, restaurants, tackle shops, and grocery and convenience stores. The Lake Palestine area was also one of the few regions that sold alcohol within a 50-mile radius, and the liquor stores supplied merchants with this needed commodity.

George Albright, Mom, and Bill in Front of His Home that Served as the Temporary Quarters for Mom and Dad After They Relocated to Texas from Los Angeles in 1974

House Built by Dad and Mom in 1982 Following Their Move to Frankston/Berryville, TX in 1974

Businesses Located in the Town Square of Frankston, Texas

Frankston Depot Library in the Town Square

Lake Palestine, with a Surface Area of Over 25,000 Acres

Sunset over Lake Palestine

For approximately 100 years, from the end of Reconstruction until the 1980s, the Democratic Party was dominant in Texas politics. The Populist Party of the late 1800s, a party that was made up of primarily poor white farmers in the South—especially North Carolina, Alabama, and Texas, in the late 19th century—provided increasing competition to the Democratic Party. The populists were hostile toward the Democrats at the time, who controlled the money and transportation industries to include banks and railroads. While the party was short-lived, and was prominent only during the 1892-96 time period, the make-up of the party and others began to form coalitions with labor unions and blacks who had been emancipated by President Lincoln, and where slavery had been banned by the Thirteenth Amendment of the Constitution. Additionally, the Fourteenth and Fifteenth Amendments ensured that all individuals born in the United States were considered citizens and had the right to vote regardless of race and color.

As a result of implementing states' rights, particularly in the South, the Democratic Party responded to the actions taken by Presidents Andrew Johnson and Ulysses S. Grant, and Congress, by ensuring its control in the South by disenfranchising most blacks, and many poor whites and Latinos, through the imposition of the poll tax and literacy tests. In the early 20th century, the poll tax was a fee required of these individuals to vote, which most could not pay. Likewise, literacy tests were administered disproportionately to blacks and other poor voters who couldn't prove a certain level of education. The end result was the disenfranchisement of these individuals from the full protection of the Constitution, thereby creating fundamentally "white primaries" in the South during elections—elections where whites primarily voted. These primaries were enforced with violence through the actions of the Ku Klux Klan and similar groups which refused to accept that people of color were equal to whites. This environment and the practices therein continued for several decades.

Things began to change, however, with the election of Franklin Delano Roosevelt (FDR) in 1933. While there was much controversy and opposition to his policies by conservatives and others, there is little doubt that the New Deal, the theme of the policies FDR put in place, was a benefit to African-Americans. Aid to blacks prior to 1933, especially in the South, had been nearly nonexistent. However, on the heels of the Great Depression, and to counter the disenfranchisement of blacks and other poor people in the South, the federal help that did come with the New Deal included programs sponsored by agencies such as the Federal Emergency Relief Administration (FERA), the Works Projects Administration (WPA), and the Civilian Conservation Corps (CCC). The WPA in particular was the largest and most ambitious New Deal agency, employing millions of unemployed people, mostly unskilled men, to carry out public works projects, including the construction of public buildings, roads and bridges. Roosevelt's approach toward civil rights legislation, however, was complicated. He spoke out against lynching, found the poll tax reprehensible, and, at the prodding of his wife, Eleanor Roosevelt, met in the White House with African-American civil rights leaders to discuss the status of blacks in the United States. On the other hand, he refused to push for anti-lynching and other similar legislation as he thought that would cost him the votes of Southerners in Congress—support he desperately needed for re-election.

World War II, which lasted from 1939 – 1945, accelerated many of the trends African-Americans were experiencing. Blacks continued to move from rural areas to cities, and more than half a million moved to the North and West during the war years. The war brought a surge in public and private spending, which in turn spurred job creation and a full-employment economy. Blacks were able to reap some of the benefits from this booming economy by obtaining more and better jobs. On the civil rights front, blacks achieved some success as well. A. Philip Randolph, a significant player in the civil rights and labor movements, threatened the Roosevelt administration in 1941 with a 100,000 person "March on Washington" if discrimination was not ended in the military and the defense industry. In response, Roosevelt issued an Executive Order in 1941 creating a Fair Employment Practices Commission (FEPC) to enforce non-discriminatory practices in employment on the basis of race, creed, color, or national origin in the defense industry and the government.

As a result of FDR's actions, blacks abandoned their historic allegiance to the Republican Party, the party of Abraham Lincoln, and moved in large numbers over to the Democrats, the party of

FDR, where they have been ever since. The Dabners made this transition, with the exception of George, Jr. who never voted for a democratic presidential candidate. He remained loyal to the Republican Party. Given the poll tax and literacy test requirements of the South, the remainder of the Dabner clan did not vote until they left the South and relocated either to Philadelphia in 1943—or Los Angeles in 1942, in the case of Mom. As such, the national election held on 7 November 1944 was the first opportunity for them to vote. This election pitted FDR, running for his fourth term as president, against Thomas E. Dewey, the Republican candidate for the presidency.

After Mother Dear moved to Philadelphia and registered to vote, she volunteered for the Democratic Party and supported the "get out the vote campaign" in the city. This involvement on the part of my grandmother was another example of good citizenship and action that impressed Mom, and which she would emulate in years to come. All Dabners and Albrights who were eligible to vote did so for FDR, with the exception of George, Jr. FDR won by a landslide with 53.4% of the popular vote and 432 electoral votes. He carried 36 of the 48 states that made up the country at that time, including all of the former Confederate States that had seceded from the Union. The important reasons for the landslide were: FDR's efforts to rebound the country from the Great Depression; the country appeared to be headed toward a victory in World War II; and there was a strong desire not to change the leadership of the country while war was ongoing. He was the only president to serve more than two terms in office. FDR passed away on 12 April 1945, following his inauguration on 20 January 1945.

Following the end of World War II and the US involvement in the Korean War ending in 1953, the economy of the country was booming. Soldiers returned home from successful military victories, found employment, purchased homes in the improved housing market, and began expanding their families through an accelerated birth rate. Between 1946 and 1961, the Baby Boomer Generation was established through the addition of approximately seventy-nine million infants to the population. In 1945, the population was just under 140 million. By the end of 1961, the population had increased to 184 million, an increase of thirty-four percent.

Among the many soldiers returning home from the war were hundreds of thousands of black soldiers who had served their country well and were champions of democracy. Among them, for example, were the Tuskegee Airmen, who reportedly never lost any Air Force bomber while escorting them over Europe. Approximately 1.5 million black soldiers served in uniform during the war in a segregated military. They returned to a society that treated them as second-class citizens. Many of these heroes who fought for their country, joined the majority of blacks in the United States still living in the Jim Crow South despite the great migration of black southerners who relocated to the North and West. Blacks in southern states continued to be forced to utilize segregated public parks, restaurants, theaters, sporting events, beaches, hospitals, schools, and public transportation. Soldiers and civilians from the South who supported the war directly in the military or through employment with defense-oriented companies, and who were exposed to the non-Jim Crow North and West or fought on European battlegrounds, were not ready to return to the southern United States and accept the status quo. One returning black soldier remarked, "It was the French who made a profound difference in my life. The French had a certain kind of openness and warmth that they exhibited towards minorities that was just unexplainable. You wouldn't know you were black when you were in their company."

The expectations of blacks and other groups for more civil rights, and who also now had the power of the vote, had a profound effect on the federal government, the country's judicial system, and public opinion. While a number of considerable achievements in the civil rights arena can be cited, six stand out in my opinion: 1) President Truman's Executive Order No. 9981 of 1948 desegregated the Armed Forced of the United States. While opposition to the order existed within the ranks of the military itself, it had a tremendous impact on the military, and in the short run, impacted the outcome of the Korean War—heavy casualties forced segregated units to merge for survival. This can be construed as the "Foxhole" concept in which one soldier has the gun and another has bullets. Working together regardless of race helped both to survive. 2) Brown v. Board of Education, a landmark case heard by United States Supreme Court in 1954 in which the Court declared state laws establishing separate public schools for black and white students unconstitutional. The Court's unanimous (9–0) decision stated that "separate educational facilities are inherently unequal," and was ruled a violation of the Equal Protection Clause of the Fourteenth Amendment of the Constitution. 3) Rosa Parks' refusal to obey a white bus driver's order to give up her seat in the colored section of the bus to a white passenger, after the white section was filled, was the spark that ignited what many consider the modern day civil rights movement. Parks' act of defiance on 1 December 1955, and the subsequent Montgomery Bus Boycott, became important symbols of the Movement, and presented Martin Luther King, Jr. with the opportunity to lead the movement and take it to demonstrable and unparalleled heights. 4) The Civil Rights Act of 1964 is a landmark piece of civil rights legislation in the United State that outlawed discrimination based on race, color, religion, sex, or national origin. It was designed to end unequal application of voter registration requirements and racial segregation in schools, at the workplace, and by facilities that served the general public. The act was signed into law by then President Lyndon Johnson, who, after signing it, reportedly turned to his press secretary and lamented that Democrats "have lost the South for a generation." He was not only correct, but his prediction lasted much longer. President Johnson, who hailed from Texas and served as both a congressman and senator for the state, was convinced that the South and particularly Texas would become increasingly Republican on both the local and state levels over the ensuing years. 5) The Twenty-Fourth Amendment to the Constitution enacted in 1964 expressly prohibited both Congress and the states from conditioning the right to vote in federal elections on payment of a poll tax or other types of tax. At the time of this amendment's passage, five states still retained a poll tax: Alabama, Arkansas, Mississippi, Texas, and Virginia. The amendment made the poll tax unconstitutional in regard to federal elections. However, it was not until 1966 that the US Supreme Court ruled that poll taxes for state elections were unconstitutional because they violated the Equal Protection Clause of the Fourteenth Amendment. 6) The Voting

Rights Act of 1965 is a landmark piece of federal legislation that prohibits discrimination in voting. It was also signed into law by President Johnson, and Congress later amended the Act five times to expand its protection. Designed to enforce the voting rights guaranteed by the Fourteenth and Fifteenth Amendments to the Constitution, the Act allowed for a mass enfranchisement of racial minorities throughout the country, especially in the South. According to many, the Act is widely considered to be the most effective piece of civil rights legislation ever enacted in the country. The Act specifically outlaws literacy tests and similar devices that were historically used to disenfranchise people of color and poor whites. In 2013, the Supreme Court, by a vote of 5 to 4, lessened some of the impact of the 1965 Act by allowing states, mostly in the South, to change their election laws without receiving federal approval in advance. Shortly after the decision, Texas announced that a voter identification law that had been blocked would go into effect immediately, and that redistricting maps would no longer need federal approval.

There is much argument about the reasons many of the Southern Democrats—or Dixiecrats, as they are sometimes called—became Republicans. Some contend that it was due to race and the civil rights legislation that was passed in the 1950s and '60s. Others argue that the shift was caused by the perceived "big government policies" of the Democrats and had nothing to do with race. Nevertheless, the shift did occur. According to the 2010 census, the cities of Frankston and Berryville both have around twenty percent registered Democrats, a Republican representation of approximately thirty percent, and an Independent percentage of fifty. These Independents tend to vote Republican in most elections. On a national level, and for the 1960 election when Democrat John Kennedy ran against Republican Richard Nixon, Kennedy won the state of Texas. In large part, this was due to Lyndon Johnson running as Kennedy's vice presidential candidate. 1.17 million Democrats outvoted the 1.12 million Republicans who voted in the state. In comparison, the 2000 presidential race between Republican George Bush and Democrat Al Gore turned out to be significantly different. 3.7 million Republicans outvoted the 2.4 million Democrats who voted in the state. Like Johnson, Bush also hailed from Texas, and was its governor between 1995 and 2000. The last Democrat to carry Texas while winning the presidency was Jimmy Carter in 1976. On the state level and from 1874 – 1979, all governors of the state were from the Democratic Party. Since 1979, four of the last six governors have been Republican. In the last twenty years, the only Democrat to hold a state-wide position in Texas was Ann Richards, who was governor between 1991 and 1995.

The creation of a pearl is a sensational occurrence in nature. Unlike gemstones and precious metals, which must be mined from the earth, pearls are developed by live oysters far below the surface of the ocean. Gemstones must be cut and polished to bring about their luster and value, with the increasing number of facets cut into any particular gemstone usually increasing its value. Pearls, on the other hand, receive no such treatment. They are completely developed within the shells of the oysters, and possess a subtle glow and beauty unlike any other gem on earth.

Both natural and cultured pearls begin their lives as a foreign object, such as a piece of grit or shell that lodges itself in an oyster's inner body where it cannot be expelled. The only difference between the two is that a natural pearl has its foreign object inserted naturally, and a cultured pearl has its object implanted by a person. The oyster begins to secrete a smooth, hard crystalline substance around the object or irritant in order to protect itself. This substance is referred to as "nacre." And as long as the irritant remains in the body of the oyster, it will continue to produce nacre around it, layer by layer. Over time, the irritant or foreign object will be encased by the silky crystalline coatings, with the result being a beautiful, highly valuable, and cherished gem called a pearl. Nature has created a miracle.

While the most popular pearls are white, they come in a variety of colors, sizes, and shapes depending on where in world they are harvested. They can be found in saltwater and in freshwater. Natural pearls, for example, are extremely rare and were historically found in the Persian Gulf. Saltwater pearls, including the Akoya cultured pearls, are grown in Japanese and Chinese waters. They are usually white or cream in color and round in shape. Australia, Indonesia, and the Philippines produce the South Sea pearl, the largest of all the pearls, and can be naturally white, cream, or golden in color. Tahitian pearls are grown in several of the islands of French Polynesia, including Tahiti. They are naturally colored pearls collectively called black pearls, but their colors include gray, blue, green, and purple. Freshwater pearls are grown in freshwater lakes, rivers, and ponds predominantly in China. Although many are white, they can also be produced in various shapes and in an array of pastel colors. Finally, many freshwater cultured pearls are grown in pearl farms.

Like the development of natural and cultured pearls that occur on the floor of the earth's seas and lakes, Mom's development began in Shreveport, Louisiana, continued in Los Angeles, and finally hit its apex over time in East Texas. And like the foreign object or irritant that is needed to start the birth of a pearl in an oyster, the irritant that was inserted into Mom was Dad's desire to relocate back to his birthplace, and the reluctant decision she made to follow her life partner. She went kicking and screaming, wondering what her life would be like in the "country." And this would be further exacerbated by the decision to sell the home in Los Angeles after my move to the Washington, DC area in 1975. Mom's safety net was gone. At times, I didn't think the marriage would last. But year after year following their move to Berryville in 1974, it appeared that the East Texas community of Berryville had become comfortable to mom. She was already a "Pearl" by name, and had shown some of her "colors" in Louisiana and California, but now East Texas was adding the coatings of its offerings that began to remove the irritant from Mom. Of course, this was coupled with Mom's desire to survive, stay active, and hopefully have an impact on her new environment. In the final analysis, she reciprocated by secreting her own form of nacre through the demonstration of her talents and unselfish contributions to the community.

The relocation of Mom and Dad to East Texas occurred during the expansion of Berryville and it proved very beneficial. While their first ten years in the area were primarily centered on enhancing my grandfather's house, building a new home, raising cattle, planting fruit trees and a vegetable garden, worshiping at Mt. Olive Sand Flat Baptist Church (est. 1898) and managing Dad's bout with colon cancer in 1979, that decade laid the foundation for what was next to come in terms of Mom's civic and community involvement. They were establishing roots in the area, and Mom began to see the environmental fruits it had to offer. It would have been easy for the two of them to maintain the lifestyle they were living, but that was not their character or makeup. As Dad would tell Gerald and me on numerous occasions, "You just can't do nothing, you have to do something." Mom was a big believer in this doctrine.

One evening in 1984, Mom and Dad dined out at the Coffee Landing Restaurant, an establishment that opened earlier that year. Located on Lake Palestine and specializing in seafood, it was the largest restaurant in the area with a footprint of 14,000 square feet and a seating capacity of about 450 that could easily satisfy the needs of many individuals and modest banquets. Folks traveled from as far as Dallas to consume the restaurant's fare. The owner of the restaurant, Tony Herrington, was from the area and had invested in a number of ventures including land, car dealerships, motels, and now this restaurant in 1984. My Grandmother Mozell had once ironed Tony's clothes to earn money, and because of this relationship, Mom and Dad quickly established a friendship with the owner of Coffee Landing.

On this particular evening, Tony came over to the table where Mom and Dad were eating and struck up a conversation. As usual, the restaurant was full as Dad observed and he shared with Tony that "business is looking great." Tony responded in the affirmative, but added that while he had plenty of cooks, waiters, and waitresses, he had no one to help him handle the business aspects of the enterprise. At this point Mom spoke up and asked what he needed. Tony said he needed an office manager who would maintain the books, make bank deposits, process payroll, pay taxes, and keep the insurances current, among other tasks. Mom declared that she could assist him, and desired to take on a part-time job to keep busy and earn income.

She and Tony arranged to meet again so she could share her background and skills. These skills were acquired while living in Los Angeles. In addition to managing a dry cleaning business with her first husband, Mom provided the leadership to establish the Beulah Baptist Church Federal Credit Union in 1958, and she managed it for fifteen years. She also managed a second credit union in Compton, CA for a couple of years. Tony Herrington was clearly impressed with Mom's credentials and experience, and in 1985 he hired her as his office manager. She worked for him for several years, but "could have remained for as long as she wanted," Tony said. "You didn't have to worry about your money. Mattie was extremely honest—she wouldn't take a dime. A lot of cash was handled on a weekly basis because of the large number of patrons at the restaurant. She paid taxes, made deposits, handled payroll, and the books were always in excellent shape. She was a good loyal employee. She took care of her job, my job and my money. No one could have asked for more."

Both Mom and Dad benefitted from being relatively unknown in the Frankston/Berryville area. Mom was not known at all except by a few family members who met her during our yearly sojourns to the area from Los Angeles in the 1950s and '60s. And even though Dad had been born in the area, he had been away for thirty-three years while living on the West Coast. Residents in the area had to take them at face value, and the two of them didn't suffer from the "Peyton Place Syndrome," a condition of many small towns where citizens are aware of their neighbors' "baggage" and draw conclusions through the rumor mill. There was little Albright baggage to judge. As such, and as an African-American woman living in this community, the role Mom was playing at Coffee Landing was a very rare occurrence, if not a first. To the best of anyone's memory, no man or woman of color had been placed in the position of handling the money and books of local businessmen, and representing them in meetings with bankers and other financial experts. Mom's reputation as a trustworthy office manager and businesswoman began to spread, and she was employed on a part-time basis by the Midway Package (liquor) Store for several years to perform the same role she performed for Tony Herrington.

Mom's abilities as an office manager and bookkeeper were affirmed by Ray Blevins, certified public accountant, who worked with the Albrights and particularly Mom over the years on a family project, when we were considering the development of a residential housing community on some of the family's property in Berryville. According to Ray, "There are very few people that you encounter in your life like Mattie Albright. Working for Tony Herrington shows she had a propensity to discern what was needed in a business environment. I was very comfortable discussing financial matters, and she had a very good grasp of everything I said. Never did I overwhelm her with a financial-related question. There is a lot of cost accounting in the development business and she had absolutely no problem with any of it. Even though she did not have an accounting degree, it didn't matter, she had the mind of an accountant. As such, it was always fun discussing financial matters with her."

By the early 1980s, it was clear that Mom was ready to get involved in more activities in the community in which she now lived. She had helped Dad recuperate into good health, she had a new home, was spending time canning vegetables and preserving peaches and pears, and had a couple of part-time jobs to earn income. She strongly believed in President Abraham Lincoln's statement made during his second inaugural address that "with malice toward none, with charity for all, with firmness in the right as God gives us to see the right…." Mom was also greatly influenced by the governor and senator of her home state of Louisiana in the 1930s, Huey P. Long, whose policies and programs greatly benefitted the "common" folk of the state, regardless of race. Finally, her mother was a great role model for her. She began helping out with food pantries that were already established through local churches to feed the elderly and the poor. She later started the Meals on Wheels program in the area and operated it for a number of years. This program is the oldest and largest organization providing senior nutritional programs. With a dedicated army of over two million volunteers in the country, nutritious meals and safety checks are provided to 2.5 million seniors in their own homes each year. After establishing a relationship with Grace Donnelly who lived down the road from her, Mom was able to convince her to support the program in Berryville. Grace willingly agreed to do so and after some time, took over the management of the program.

The charity work Mom was performing, coupled with her part-time positions, was providing her a growing understanding of the needs of Berryville and Frankston. She was establishing excellent relationships with both town leaders and residents alike. She was a black woman and a Democrat living in a community where the population was over ninety percent white and largely Republican-leaning. She began attending the meetings of the Berryville City Council as an interested citizen. She listened intently and contributed to the discussions as appropriate. She supplemented her knowledge by reading the Frankston Citizen, the weekly newspaper for the area. And on a daily basis, she watched Fox News, the national conservative news program, as well as the East Texas news programs. Council members and the mayor quickly observed her ability to understand many of the issues the city was facing and the ideas she generated to overcome them. She was approached about running for an open seat on the council, and agreed to compete for it.

The council is made up of five council members and a mayor. Members and the mayor each serve a two-year term and there is no limit on the number of terms. The terms are staggered to facilitate continuity in the handling of the city's business. Members must live in Berryville for at least six months before running for the council. The mayor has to have lived in Berryville for a year. In February of each year, the mayor calls for an election of council members and for the mayoral opening, if necessary, to be held usually on the second Saturday in May of every year. This call is announced in the Legal section of the *Frankston Citizen*. Those citizens who want to run fill out an application. A drawing is held to determine how their names will be listed on the ballot. An election judge is appointed from the Council along with a clerk. Citizens request a ballot by mail or can visit the city hall and vote early. About 75% of the eligible voters actually vote each year.

Mom was easily elected in 1986 and served in this capacity until her retirement in 2002. In 1991, she took on the role as the Mayor Pro Tem of Berryville and served in this capacity until 1996. In this role, she fulfilled the duties of the mayor when he was unable to do so. At the time, Mayor James Colvin traveled extensively, and Mom would step in to run the council meetings and perform other duties as needed. Given her business background, she was regularly called upon to make important business decisions in the mayor's absence, including the approval of purchase requisitions and the distribution of payments. There were no specified duties assigned to the Mayor Pro Tem position. The council, however, would form a committee from time to time to work on a particular problem the community was facing.

Mayor Colvin recalled working with Mom on the ordinances having to do with cleaning up the city. One of the objectives was to clean up the Holiday Hills section of Berryville. This area was considered undesirable and had to be improved in order to make it attractive for both current and future residents. The area had become a haven for drug dealers, and some residents were not storing their trash properly. In fact, some would throw trash out of their windows or onto the roads. This prompted the mayor and city council to institute a mandatory trash pickup policy and add an incremental charge to the monthly water bill. According to Sharyn Harrison, the city manager, "That decision caused a big stink. Many residents were very much opposed to the change, but they were also the ones who threw thrash on the sides of the streets. In the end it all worked out, and Mattie was a key contributor to this outcome. She had a very calming effect on folks. Residents, who are usually resistant to change, didn't want any more charges added to their water bills. But during council meetings, Mattie explained the problems and goals to be achieved so thoroughly that within six months of the council's decision, it secured the acceptance of all citizens. One of the biggest opponents to the decision visited the city hall a year later to 'eat crow' and declare that the move to have the trash picked up was the best thing the city ever did. He initially thought it would be chaotic, but in the end it worked out wonderfully."

Mayor Colvin also noted that Mom helped him with his re-election as mayor. "She was so involved in everything having to do with the city business, folks just wore her out. Consequently, in her later years on the council, Mattie didn't serve on committees. But even if she wasn't on a committee, and if you wanted to get something done and needed her input, you called her. She knew who was best to get a particular project accomplished." He further exclaimed that "Mattie could well have been mayor, I can tell you that. Everybody in the town would have voted for her, but she didn't want the position."

While Mom's contributions to Berryville and Frankston through both her civic and charitable involvements were extremely notable, she also realized that both communities had growth potential through additional commerce and the draw of Lake Palestine. A chamber of commerce, also referred to in some circles as a board of trade, is a form of business network to further the interests of businesses and the community in which they reside. Business owners in towns and cities form these local networks to advocate on behalf of the business community. Chambers elect a board of directors or executive council to set policy for the organization. The board or council then appoints a President, CEO or Executive Director, plus staffing appropriate to size, to run the organization. Even though Mom didn't work directly with a chamber while living in Los Angeles, she thought that such an organization would greatly benefit the area. She didn't have a business that would become part of the chamber, should it be formed, so her goal was entirely altruistic. She initially approached several community leaders to secure their interest and support. Among them were Bob Pickle, a constable for the area; Lillie Claybon, retired director of food services at Texas College in Tyler; and Erv Berry, former mayor of Berryville. They all endorsed the idea of establishing a chamber and pledged their support and involvement.

Mom then approached many of the businesses in Berryville and Frankston to see if they would be interested in forming a chamber to benefit them individually as well as lure additional businesses to the area. In the final analysis, twelve businesses agreed to become charter members of the Berryville Chamber of Commerce. Among them were a grocery store, a couple of auto repair shops, a car dealership, a hardware store, and a convenience store. In September 1987 the Chamber received its charter, and its nonprofit tax exempt status from the IRS.

Mom became its first president in January 1988. She and other officers of the organization were sworn in by Kenneth Davis, executive director of the chamber of commerce for Athens, Texas, a nearby town 25 miles west of Berryville and Frankston. She was elected president again in 1992. In 1988, membership in the chamber was available for businesses for an annual fee of $25.00 and the fee for an individual membership was $12.50. One year after its formation, the Chamber had grown to thirty-seven members, and held its first annual banquet at the Coffee Landing Restaurant in January 1989. Mom wanted to celebrate the chamber's existence, announce to attendees the progress made during the year, and honor specific individuals among its membership. Included in the advancements made was the establishment of an Industrial Committee to "encourage industrial growth in the area near Lake Palestine."

Also notable was her genius in recognizing not only elected officials in the area, but more importantly, deserving citizens who contributed much in either the roles they played for the community or through their charitable work. Among these were Educator of the Year, Police and Fire Persons of the Year, Business Person of the Year, and Citizen of the Year. These acts not only popularized the Chamber, but brought about cohesiveness among the citizens, many of whom attended the banquets to add their appreciation to those being honored. Given the growth in the size of the Berryville Chamber after its first year, committees were created to provide focus and attention in a variety of areas including retail, membership, legislative, youth and education, industrial and community development, tourism, and leadership and motivation. Mom wanted to adapt the activities of the chamber to the times based on what the community needed. She kept her members engaged through committee and board assignments, effectively channeled their individual strengths, and influenced them to stay focused on the chamber's priorities. She regularly polled the chamber membership to ascertain what they needed both individually and collectively. From this information innovative ideas were put into action, and organizational goals were framed. Within the first year of the creation of the chamber, for example, plans were underway for the production of a video cassette recording to promote the Frankston, Berryville, and Lake Palestine areas to businesses, industries, and individuals seeking to relocate to the area. A special committee was appointed to oversee and coordinate this project. As president of the Berryville Chamber, Mom was a member of this special committee. United Telephone of Texas offered to produce the video recording, as it would benefit from the future growth in the area. The business community in Athens, Texas had produced a similar video recording a few years earlier, and had much reported success. There has been steady growth in Berryville. Between 1990 and 2012, Berryville experienced a population growth of 33 percent, and there are in excess of 6000 residents in the overall Lake Palestine area.

Neighboring cities heard of the work of the newly formed chamber and wanted to get in on the action. In 1994, the Berryville Chamber became a division of the Lake Palestine Area Chamber of Commerce, and Mom became its first president for that year. She was seventy-seven years old, and still had energy in her tank at that point of taking on the responsibilities of the position. What was once an organization of a dozen businesses in Berryville increased over time to approximately one hundred members in the cities of Berryville, Frankston, Flint, Poynor, Cuney, Bullard, Noonday, LaRue, and Coffee City. As she did to perform her role for the credit unions, Mom converted part of the den at her home into an office area, inclusive of a desk and filing cabinets to handle the Chamber's business.

Another of her significant contributions was to help raise revenue for Berryville for various community-related projects under the auspices of the Chamber, since franchise taxes from cable usage and the water system were the only sources of income for the city. This led to the establishment of the annual Blue Grass Festival which began in 1989. Blue grass music was not high on Mom's list of music to listen to. She preferred the big band music of the 1930s and '40s, as well as blues and the R & B music of the '60s. And, of course, music produced and played by her son Gerald was always at the top. However, Mom's preferences became low on the totem pole when it came to the needs and desires of the residents of Berryville. She was a good listener. Blue grass music was the order of the day, and a festival was sponsored featuring that genre of music. It was a hit for the community and lasted for three years. Money raised via the festival was used for Chamber and community-oriented projects. Particularly noteworthy was the production of a detailed Berryville area map that illustrated all roads, Lake Palestine, and other places of interest that would promote the city to individuals and businesses alike.

As Ray Blevins noted, "Mattie was a great leader. She demonstrated a tremendous depth of leadership. She was not afraid to organize a plan on anything she put her mind to, and then bring others along who believed in her vision. One of the biggest contributions she made to the community was her passion for things that mattered. She was called into what was given to her as gifts that would make the community better. This was infectious to me and I couldn't help but feel that it had to be infectious to all around her. She was also interested in those things that would improve the community in the long term. Whatever

Mattie decided to work on, she would see it to completion. Even when it became difficult due to health reasons, she would take her time and use her great attention to detail and persevered until the project was completed. She did not want to leave anything undone. Mattie was also a great communicator. Never did I have any problems with understanding what she wanted to do or where she wanted to go with a project. She could take abstract thoughts and reduce them to straightforward concrete items and make them work. She was a very transparent individual—what you saw is what you got. Part of this was her maturity in her faith and part of it was her maturity in knowing herself. She wouldn't pull any punches, nothing was concealed in her communication style, and she never missed an opportunity to help you in your life's journey. Not only did she understand herself, but over time, she understood those around her and what made them tick. She used this effectively to engage others in her vision. This was not done maliciously, but more to assist them and the community at large. "

James Colvin succeeded mom as President of the Lake Palestine Area Chamber, and also served as the Mayor of Berryville and on the city council. "Many individuals approached me about getting involved in the Chamber and the Council and I refused them. But it was different when Mattie approached me. I was in Huntsville, Alabama when she called and asked if I would be president of the chamber. I could not refuse her. When I returned from the trip, I was the newly elected president of the area-wide chamber in 1995. Next, there was a council seat that became available as a result of someone leaving, and I was approached again by several individuals and I declined.

Along came Mattie, and I ended up on the city council, and subsequent to this, I was voted in as mayor. Sharyn Harrison, Berryville City Manager, asked me once 'How is Mattie getting you to do all of this—does she have something on you?' I told her that 'I just could not turn her down. She is such a strong leader and I just enjoy working with her.'"

Joe Tindel, the former owner of Frankston's newspaper, *The Frankston Citizen*, met Mom in the mid '70s, and had a number of interactions with her through the newspaper coverage of the Berryville City Government and the Berryville and Lake Palestine Chambers of Commerce. His impressions of Mom were very similar to those of James Colvin. "Mattie was very forthright in everything she pursued. She never equivocated and was very resolute. I never got the impression that something couldn't be done if Mattie wanted it to get done. I was very impressed with how much she was willing to give to the community. She was largely responsible for the progress that various organizations made, such as the Chambers of Commerce. She was an out-standing leader of the Berryville City Council and was effective as Mayor Pro-Tem. She was always forward-looking and constantly wanting to improve the conditions of people and the community at-large. I have no reservations in saying she was very important to the community. The community has missed her influence since she passed away. There are others who have filled leadership roles in Berryville, but to fill Mattie's shoes is very hard to do."

Lillie Claybon, the only other African-American on both chambers of commerce, praised Mom immensely. "She was a good

community worker, and when she ran things, they were right—
one could not turn her down. She was a community leader and
a great mentor to many."

Over the years, Mom received a number of awards for the contributions she made to the organizations and communities she
supported. Among these are the following: Service award for
serving as the manager treasurer for the Beulah Baptist Church
Federal Credit Union for fifteen years; President's Award from
the Berryville Chamber of Commerce; Outstanding Citizen
of the Year Award from the Lake Palestine Area Chamber
of Commerce; Lifetime Membership Award from the Lake
Palestine Area Chamber of Commerce; An Outstanding Older
Texan Award from Governor Ann W. Richards; Outstanding
Volunteer Service Award from the Texas Department on Aging
and Governor Ann W. Richards; and the State of Texas House of
Representatives Award for receiving the Lifetime Membership
Award from the Lake Palestine Area Chamber of Commerce.

MARCH 30
1974

-TO-

MATTIE PEARL ALBRIGHT

IN APPRECIATION OF
FIFTEEN YEARS
OF
UNEXCELLED SERVICE AS
"MANAGER-TREASURER"
-OF THE-

BEULAH BAPTIST FEDERAL
CREDIT UNION

Coffee Landing Restaurant Where Mom Worked in the Mid-'80s

25¢ **THE FRANKSTON CITIZEN**

PER COPY

A Newspaper Dedicated to Community Service

78th YEAR—32nd WEEK   FRANKSTON, ANDERSON COUNTY, TEXAS 75763 THURSDAY, FEBRUARY 4, 1988   USPS 208-820   ESTABLISHED 1910

Berryville Chamber of Commerce begins work with installation

BERRYVILLE—The new Berryville Chamber of Commerce board of directors will jump right off into the work of their organization Thursday at 7 p.m. at City Hall after enjoying an officer installation dinner Saturday night at Coffee Landing Restaurant.

Officers and board members were installed by Kenneth Davis, executive director of the Athens Chamber of Commerce.

CHAMBER PRESIDENT—Mrs. W.D. [Mattie] Albright takes the oath of office as the first president of the newly-organized Berryville Chamber of Commerce. Kenneth Davis, executive director of the Athens Chamber of Commerce, installed the officers Saturday night at a dinner meeting at Coffee Landing Restaurant.   —CITIZEN PHOTO

Mom being sworn in as the first president of the Berryville Chamber of Commerce

PRESIDENT'S AWARD

BERRYVILLE
CHAMBER of COMMERCE

1988 ~ 1989

Mattie Albright

THE FRANKSTON CITIZEN

A Newspaper Dedicated to Community Service

25¢ Per Copy

79th YEAR—50th WEEK   FRANKSTON, ANDERSON COUNTY, TEXAS 75763 THURSDAY, JANUARY 25, 1990   USPS 208-620   ESTABLISHED 1910

CERTIFICATES PRESENTED — Certificates of Appreciation were presented to a number of members of the Berryville Chamber of Commerce in the chamber's annual membership banquet Saturday night at Coffee Landing Restaurant. Entertainment was presented by Joyce Shipp, third from left, Smith County Home Demonstration Agent. Among those receiving certificates were, left to right, treasurer Margaret (Boots) Hellig, president Mattie Albright, immediate past vice president Evie Wiggins, Mayor E.H. Berry and incoming vice president J.R. (Bob) Pickle. Also receiving certificates were Carter Eggen, secretary Agnes Steifer and James E. Berry, founder of Berryville.

—CITIZEN PHOTO

Berryville chamber gives appreciation certificates

COFFEE CITY—Several Berryville Chamber of Commerce members along with other city residents were given certificates of appreciation for their efforts here Saturday night.

The awards were presented during the second annual Berryville Chamber of Commerce membership banquet.

Certificates were presented to chamber president Mattie Albright, new vice president J.R. (Bob) Pickle, outgoing vice president Evie Wiggins, treasurer Margaret (Boots) Hellig, secretary Agnes Steifer, Berryville Mayor E.H. Berry, Berryville founder James E. Berry and board member.

Entertainment for the evening was presented by Joyce Shipp, home demonstration agent for Smith County. She presented a humorous program using hats which depicted various kinds of personality traits. Mrs. Shipp is the wife of Frankston girls' basketball coach Roy Shipp, sister of Supt. Bill Alexander and daughter of J.L. Alexander of Berryville.

Chamber President Mrs. Albright reviewed the chamber's work during the last year and outlined plans for the coming year.

She noted that the chamber plans to sponsor the second annual Summer Bluegrass Festival which will be held at the Lenore Berry Park at Berryville. On the program

will be the Sullivans from Alabama, Shady Grove Ramblers and the Joe Featherston Country Travelers.

Special recognition was given to out-of-town guests from Athens and Tyler as well as the Frankston area.

The chamber recently elected three new directors. They are J.R. (Bob) Pickle, Ruth Cozzer and Joe Reed, who will serve three year terms.

The chamber now has 37 members.

Other board members are Dave Lockwood and Bill Alexander.

The Chamber of Commerce board meets the first Thursday of each month and anyone is invited to attend the meeting.

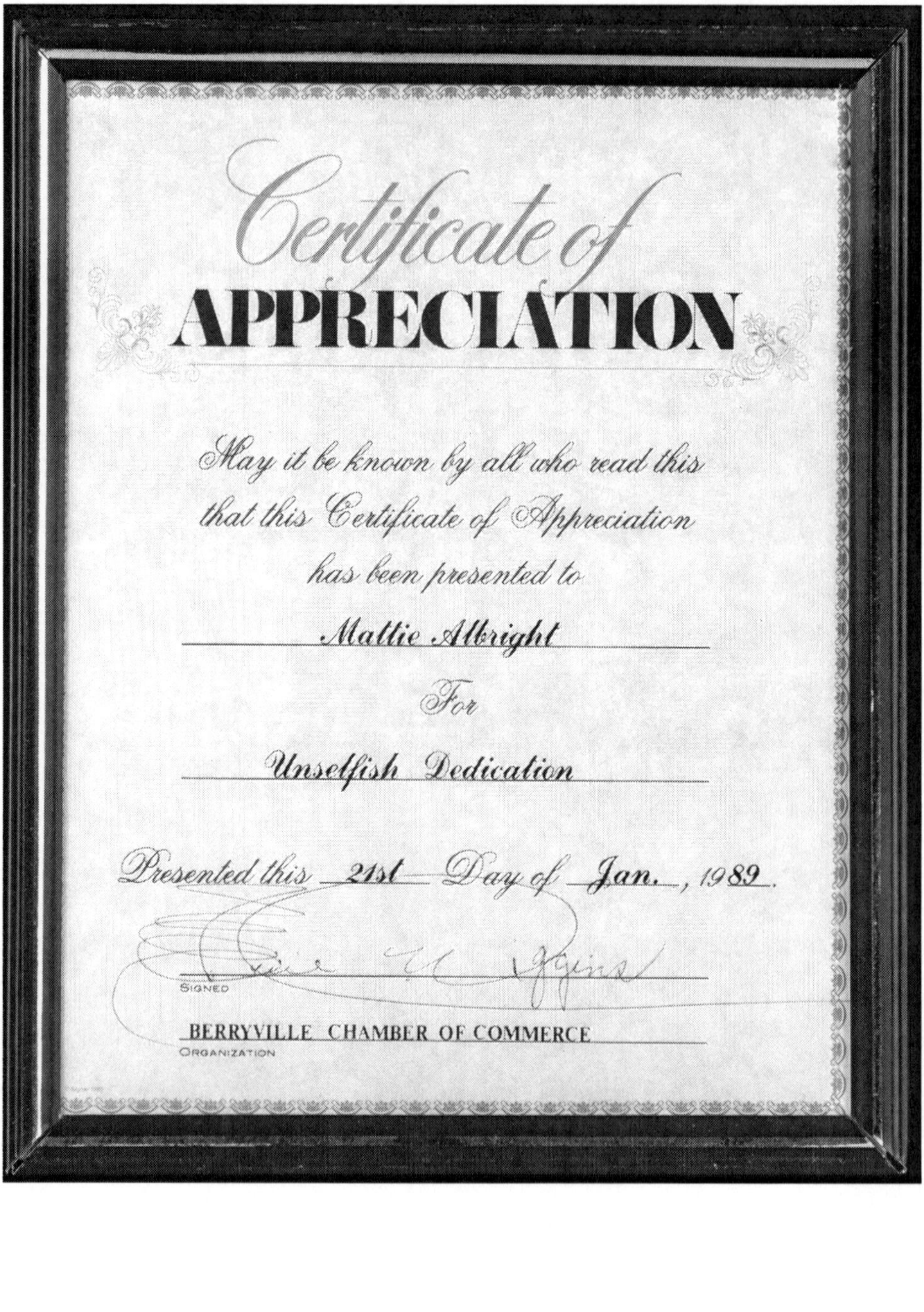

Certificate of
APPRECIATION

May it be known by all who read this

that this Certificate of Appreciation

has been presented to

Mattie Albright

For

Unselfish Dedication

Presented this __21st__ Day of __Jan.__, 1989.

BERRYVILLE CHAMBER OF COMMERCE

BLUEGRASS FESTIVAL—A large crowd turned out Saturday night despite the threat of showers for the annual Bluegrass Festival sponsored by the Berryville Chamber of Commerce. Among the groups enjoyed by those present was the Sullivans of Alabama, performing here around dusk at Lenore Berry Park. Proceeds went to help finance various community projects. —CITIZEN PHOTO

Residents Enjoying the Berryville Blue Grass Festival in 1989

VIDEO PROMOTION PLANNED—A group of Frankston and Lake Palestine area community leaders met with United Telephone of Texas representatives Thursday night to kick off planning for a videocassette recording featuring the benefits of this area for business and industrial location. Among those present were, left to right, J.R. (Bob) Pickle of Poynor, Charlie Pagitt of Poynor, Mrs. Mattie Albright of Berryville, LaPoynor Supt. Doug Steger of Poynor, United Telephone public relations manager LaNelle Clement, economic development manager Rick Brown, community relations administrator Jim Kite, the Rev. Lee Lamb of Frankston, Rusty Blair of Frankston and Coffee City and Frankston School Supt. Bill Alexander.　　　—CITIZEN PHOTO

An
Outstanding
Older
Texan

Presented in recognition of your personal dedication to creating a better quality of life for your fellow citizens. As a senior member of your community, you possess unique qualities that have made your advice and counsel particularly valuable: knowledge, perspective, practical experience and the leadership ability that comes only with time. Through your generous contributions of these and other qualities, you have helped to enrich the lives of today's Texans—and those yet to come.

THE TEXAS DEPARTMENT ON AGING

Ann W. Richards

Governor of Texas

Mattie Albright

May 26th, 1994.

Mary Tapp

Executive Director
Texas Department on Aging

OUTSTANDING VOLUNTEER SERVICE

TDoA
TEXAS DEPARTMENT ON AGING

Presented to

MATTIE ALBRIGHT

As an expression of our sincere gratitude for your valuable contributions of time, energy, expertise and goodwill in volunteer work for your community

Ann W. Richards
Governor of Texas

Mary Lapp
Executive Director
Texas Department on Aging

Mattie P. Albright

OUTSTANDING CITIZEN
OF THE YEAR
AWARD

1994

LAKE PALESTINE AREA
CHAMBER of COMMERCE

25¢

Per Copy

THE FRANKSTON

A Newspaper Dedicated to Communi

VOLUME 85—NO. 20   FRANKSTON, ANDERSON COUNTY, TEXAS 75763 THURSDAY, FE

CHAMBER HONORS—Mrs. Mattie Albright, center, was honored as Citizen of the Year and for her service as immediate past president by the Lake Palestine Area Chamber of Commerce Thursday night, Feb. 2 in the chamber's annual banquet. Taking over as president for 1995 was James Colvin, right of Mrs. Albright. Also recognized and installed were new directors for 1995. Left to right are Lillie Clayton, John Floyd, Evie Wiggins, Jana Eaves, Mrs. Albright, Jeff Austin III, Colvin, Odell Hinton, Kelly Boykin and Britt Bacon.   —*CITIZEN PHOTO*

Electi
for st

Frankston area voters in son County will be going to t Saturday, Feb. 11 in the spec tion to select a District 1 representative.

Three candidates have f places on the ballot in the c They are Frankston bank Austin III, Palestine realto Staples; and Lisa Harris O Oakwood rancher.

Voting will be from 7 a.m. t at the three usual area voti cinct locations.

County election officials a ers in Precinct 18 will vote Anderson County courthouse in Frankston. Box 18 voters tary School. Box 23 will be at the Brushy Creek Com Center.

The election was calle former State Rep. Elton B Montalbo was appointed stat ance commissioner by Gov. W. Bush.

W. Bush.

District 11 includes A Cherokee, Leon and Robert ties.

Early voting was held thr 7 at the Anderson Count house in Palestine. Election reported Wednesday morni 8 that 1,204 persons had

Mrs. Albright given Citizen of Year honor by C of C

LIFETIME
MEMBERSHIP
AWARD

Mattie Albright

AWARDED BY

LAKE PALESTINE AREA
CHAMBER of COMMERCE

1998

25¢

Per Copy

A Newspaper Dedicated to Community Service

VOLUME 89 — NO. 26   FRANKSTON, ANDERSON COUNTY, TEXAS 75763 THURSDAY, JANUARY 14, 1999   USPS 208-620

LPA CHAMBER AWARDS — These Lake Palestine area residents received awards Monday night, Jan. 11 during the annual banquet for the Lake Palestine Area Chamber of Commerce. Front row, left to right, are Mattie Albright of Berryville, lifetime membership award; Brooks Atwood of Frankston, receiving the Business Person of the Year award for his father, Ronald (Dick) Atwood of Atwood Hat Co.; Mary Phillips, counselor at Frankston ISD who received the Teacher/Educator of the Year Award; and Laura Tolner, 1998 president. Back row, left to right, are Hayden Mitchell of Frankston named Law Enforcement Officer of the Year; Al Buuck of Chandler, chosen Citizen of the Year; and Rob Stevens of Berryville, honored as Volunteer Firefighter of the Year. Not pictured is Louise Walding of Frankston, honored as Volunteer of the Year. — *CITIZEN PHOTO*

Al Buuck, others i
Palestine Area Cha

COFFEE CITY — A Lake Palestine area community leader, Al Buuck of Chandler, was chosen as Citizen of the Year for 1998 during awards ceremonies Monday night, Jan. 11 at the annual banquet of the Lake Palestine Area Chamber of Commerce.

The award was one of several given area residents for their contributions during the past year.

The banquet audience also heard Dr. Rodney Mabry, president of the University of Texas at Tyler, speak on the importance of community involvement and helping others gain a higher education.

Others honored by the chamber were Rob Stevens of Berryville, Volunteer Firefighter of the Year; Mary Phillips, Frankston ISD counselor, Teacher/Educator of the Year; Louise Walding of Frankston, Volunteer of the Year; Ronald (Dick) Atwood of Atwood Hat Co. of Frankston, Business Person of the Year; Hayden Mitchell of Frankston, Law Enforcement Officer of the Year; and Mattie Albright of Berryville, Lifetime

president; Diana Hartley, seci and James Colvin, treasurer. tors are Al Buuck, Jim Hartle McKay, Lana Lust, Mel Zimm and Bob Pickle. Lillie Claybo Mattie Albright were install advisory directors.

Outgoing directors are Barry ton, Richard Boteen, Ruth G John Floyd and Mike Hender

Presenting entertainmen vocalist Tanya Hurst of White

LAKE PALESTINE AREA
CHAMBER OF COMMERCE

APPRECIATION TO

MATTIE ALBRIGHT

This is to certify that the above mentioned has been appointed

Director of the

1998

Lake Palestine Area Chamber of Commerce Board of Directors.
Duly taking office this January 19th day of 1998.

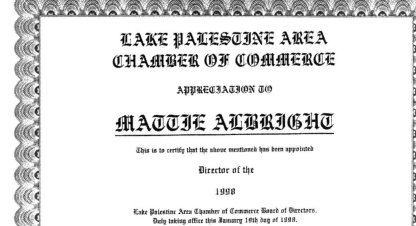

Signed: Laura Tower - 1998 President

The State of Texas
House of Representatives
The Honorable Clyde Alexander

Congratulations

MATTIE ALBRIGHT

for being honored by the

Lake Palestine Chamber of Commerce
with the
Lifetime Membership Award

I have hereunto signed my name and caused the Seal of the House of Representatives
to be affixed at the city of Austin, this the, twenty-first day of January 1999.

State Representative

Kindergarten, fifth gr...
at Frankston to grad...

Students in kindergarten and fifth grade at Frankston School will be graduated in ceremonies beginning at 8:15 a.m. Friday, May 26 in the high school auditorium.

Kindergarten students graduating include Mason Beddingfield, Chris tin Birch, Katy Boykin, Clint Bruch miller, Michael Bullard, Jeremiah Carter, Barbara Christie, Brandi Coleman, Tiara Corley, Michael Cortez, Maegan Deckert, John Dil lion, Cornelius Dixon, Nikki Dunlap, Taylor Edwards, Joshua Fields, Lee Fisher, Stephanie Fisher, Justin Flannery, Michael Foster, Kedrick Freeney, Cordero Gentry, Meric Glover, Latosha Gray, Joseph Grud za, Linsey Hanna, Michael Hatton, Oliver Hatton, Douglas Huntsberg er, José Mascorro, Carolyn Mays, Ashleigh Menninger, Bryan Mitch ell, Jacob Moss, Jarrette Neal, Heather Ness, Christopher Pickard, Kristin Pinkerton, Lucas Roberts, Stephanie Rowden, Wesley Saun ders, LaTiandra Smith, Matthew Stewart, Alex Till, Nicholas Webb, Courtney Wheeler, Jacob Whitehurst

and Ashley Woods.

Fifth grade gradu na Allen, Christopher Paul Baker, Danie Stephen Bedell, Jere Claxton, Christophe Corley, Wes Cox, Br Vance Dallas, Lynn l pher Denson, Tina D ica Dewberry, Jona Chadwick Donnell, Courtney Freeney, C Jill Guerra, Amy H Hawkins, Christophe topher Ingram, Tr Sharronn Laughlin, er, Justin Leonard, baugh, Billy Martin, Ryan McCoy, Christ Keith Medlin, Micha ryn Moseley, Sarah l di Nash, Charles N Newman, Leigh Paln lips, Isaac Roberts, Y son, Traderrin Walker Destiny Swisher, Ric Cody Tippett, Lance Welch, Sutton Willif dard and Nicole Woo

TWO-YEAR ANNIVERSARY—Members of the Lake Palestine Area Chamber of Commerce and other guests were on hand Friday morning, May 19 for a ribbon-cutting at Smokey Joe's Hickory House Barbecue. The event marked the two-year anniversary under the ownership of Joe and Mary Beard. Front row, left to right, are Lillie Claybon, Kelly Boykin, Frances M. Beard, Joe Beard, Mary Beard, chamber vice president John Floyd, Mattie Albright, Bob Pickle, Ruth Cowger and Evie Wiggins. Back row, left to right, are Ruby Hall, Ralph Hall, Laura and Don Toner, Marie Chaneyworth, Sue Mays and Rebecca Pemberton.
—*CITIZEN PHOTO*

Bullard firm apparent
low bidder on project

Frankston
School Briefs

Frankston Middle School Student Council held an end-of-school dance Saturday, May 20 with members and

FAMILY SA
Serving Frank

Representing the Chamber of Commerce, Mom Helping to Celebrate the Second Anniversary of Smokey Joe's Hickory House Barbeque Restaurant in 1995.

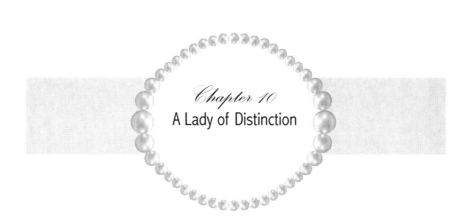

Throughout her adulthood, Mom demonstrated the values and ethics she learned from her mother, Mother Dear, and the principles of supporting and assisting her fellow human beings through the teachings delivered while she attended Central Colored High School and Antioch Baptist Church in Shreveport, Louisiana. She was independent, a survivor, and family-oriented. Her community orientation led her to function on the city council, serve as the Mayor Pro-Tem, and establish and manage a credit union and two chambers of commerce. Her belief in "charity for all" prompted her to create a Meals on Wheels Program and participate in food pantry activities that assisted the elderly and poor. She was a lady of distinction in both grace and style. According to many with whom she collaborated, Mom was beautiful both inside and out. Sharyn Harrison thought "Mattie was one of the most elegant ladies I have ever known. She always dressed nice, and her speech was professional. She was a super lady." Lillie Claybon reflected that "Mattie was a nice lady and carried herself in such a way that one had to respect her." James Colvin, former Mayor of Berryville, remembers when he first met Mom. "I was building a home in the Three Points section of Berryville. Mattie and Erv Berry (also a former mayor of Berryville) pulled up in a car. They were discussing the Blue Grass Festival Mattie was planning to hold at the recently completed ball field behind the city hall. I was so impressed with how she spoke and how beautiful and classy she was. I was amazed by her. I was new to the community and an outsider. But she befriended me and put me to work."

Mom was living a fulfilled life. She had a loving husband, two sons who had achieved success in their respective professions, grandchildren and great-grandchildren, and plenty of friends. She was serving the community and assisting those in need of help. But there still existed a void in terms of her sphere of influence and contribution—that being a genuine concern about the development of future generations, and particularly those within the black community. Just as she wanted the business community in the Lake Palestine area to thrive and prosper, so did she want the citizens in the area to thrive. Doing so would increase the visibility of the areas surrounding the Lake, and make it more attractive to potential businesspersons and other residents. To this end, Mom consulted with two of her dearest friends in the area, Dr. L.L. Marks and Lillie Claybon, to discuss the feasibility of establishing a group of young black women to whom the three of them and other volunteers would expose a variety of educational and cultural activities. The three of them agreed and approached other professionals in the area to determine if they were interested in mentoring young women. A number of them answered the call and The Cultural Interest Group (CIG) became a reality. Dr. Marks served as president and Mom took on the role as vice president. Mom hosted the first set of meetings at her home. Through the efforts of these mentors, young women were exposed to dramatic plays, symphonies, art exhibits, and the Ebony Fashion Fair. They also participated in voter registration activities and listened to renowned speakers.

Through such activities, the mentees, who numbered in the low twenties, were encouraged to develop their individual talents and pursue careers in business and the performing arts. The CIG also provided scholarships to these young women to assist them in attending local junior colleges, including Henderson County Junior College, and Tyler Junior College. Mom secured a facility at the Frankston High School to hold the first award and scholarship banquet. The CIG was successful in its mission, and word of this success began to spread. Women from the Jacksonville and Tyler areas joined the group. In 1985, CIG became part of the National Coalition of 100 Black Women, an organization with many of the same values as CIG and with a mission to meet the career needs of women and facilitate their access into mainstream America. To this end, they use the tools of role modelling and mentoring to provide meaningful guidance to young women, and reveal to them the historic and current achievements of black women.

Belinda Wallace was a member of the CIG and mentored some of the young women. In her opinion, "There were many young black females in the area who Mattie wanted to get involved in community and political activities such as voter registration, and serving the elderly and poor. Expanding their horizons was the ultimate objective. Many of them had never participated in such activities before Mattie established the Cultural Interest Group." Belinda further remarked on mom's contributions to the East Texas area in general. "The bonds Mattie created throughout the various parts of Henderson County and between counties are still ongoing, and folks remain involved in various activities. At the county fairs, for example, Mattie influenced the inclusion of art and other cultural activities to complement the food and quilting that traditionally were displayed. She was assertive but effective in her style when dealing with others. She was professional, but meant business in getting the job done. Mattie had the unique ability to make others believe that they made the decision to get involved or offer ideas when in fact, it was her influence. The community has been better because of the influence Mattie had on people."

Concurrent with her involvement with the CIG, Mom became affiliated with the Top Ladies of Distinction (TLOD), Inc. in the late '80s and early '90s. TLOD, Inc. was chartered in the state of Texas in 1964 as a non-profit educational and humanitarian organization. The organization marshaled the talents, energies, and skills of women nationally in a collaborative effort to help alleviate the moral and social problems confronting youth. The charter was later expanded to include improving the status of women, service to senior citizens, community beautification, and community partnerships. Chapters nationwide have partnered with other organizations such as the National Council of Negro Women, the National Association for the Advancement of Colored People, United Negro College Fund, Sickle Cell Disease Awareness, and the March of Dimes. Membership in TLOD has grown to include thousands of dedicated, concerned, hard-working ladies representing a cross-section of resourceful women, who work with thousands of female youth, officially known as Top Teens of America (TTA). Through interaction with these young ladies, Top Ladies endeavor to achieve the following: encourage high academic scholarship; develop social graces, leadership and fellowship abilities; develop pride in self, home and community; and encourage appreciation for their ethnic and cultural heritage. Mom now possessed a much larger platform to help influence youth in East Texas. Lady Albright, as she was fondly called in the organization, became an active member of the Rose City (Tyler) Chapter of TLOD and worked diligently as a TTA Advisor. She gave presentations at chapter meetings on educating the youth. At the age of seventy-five, she also attended the 23rd Annual Area I Conference of TLOD in 1992, and accompanied 55 chapter Top Teens and a number of her fellow "Ladies" to Houston, where the overall conference was attended by more than a thousand teens and about 300 Ladies and Lords, who are husbands to the Top Ladies.

As she did when she established the Berryville Chamber of Commerce which later grew into the Lake Palestine Area Chamber of Commerce, Mom planted the seeds that created the Cultural Interest Group, and this subsequently became part of a national organization. She also became affiliated with TLOD, which has been having a national impact on youth for years. As Ray Blevins stated, "Mattie was never looking for immediate gratification—she was interested in those things that would make the community and individuals better over a protracted period of time."

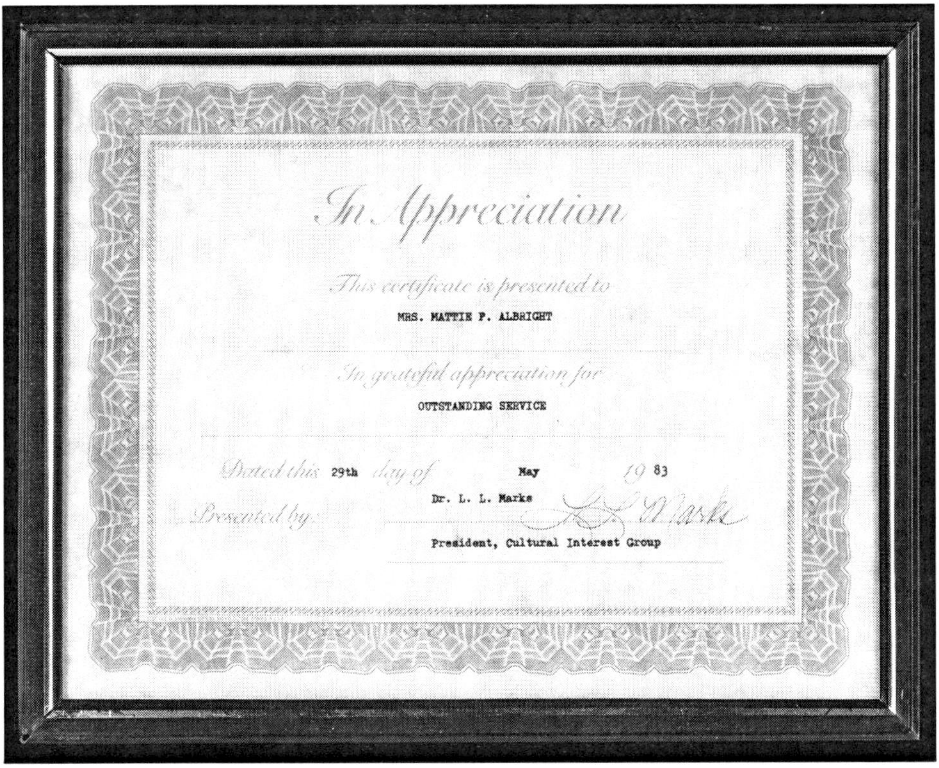

In Appreciation

This certificate is presented to

MRS. MATTIE F. ALBRIGHT

In grateful appreciation for

OUTSTANDING SERVICE

Dated this 29th *day of* May 19 83

Dr. L. L. Marks

Presented by:

President, Cultural Interest Group

Mentors Serving in the Cultural Interest Group — 1984

Chapter 11
Mattie Albright Road

On 6 May 2003, Gerald and I landed about two hours apart
at the Dallas Fort Worth International Airport (DFW). I arrived
from the Washington, DC area, and Gerald took a flight from
Los Angeles. Since I arrived first, I rented a car, hung out at the
Hilton Hotel at the airport, had lunch, and waited for a signal from Gerald that he had landed. When he did, I met him
at the terminal, and we made the two-hour drive from DFW
to Berryville. This two-hour time period gave us some time to
catch up on our respective lives and share some laughs, which
we customarily do when together. About a half hour outside of
Berryville, we stopped to change into business attire suitable
for the council meeting, as we both flew in casual clothing.
When we arrived at the city hall, our timing was perfect, as the
business portion of the council meeting was about to conclude.
Upon entering the meeting room, Mom's and Dad's eyes nearly
popped from their heads, and they looked with amazement as
we took our seats next to them, wondering how we pulled off
this surprise.

The room was filled with sixty-five attendees, many more than
the five to ten who usually attended council meetings. The topic
of property taxes was not on the meeting agenda that always
caused a big draw of residents. Mayor James Colvin began the
recognition and awards portion of the meeting by welcoming

all attendees and newcomers, giving a thorough description of the many contributions made to the community by Mattie and Grace, and he presented them with their respective plaques. The mayor was then followed by Mayor Pro Tem Oris Gary, who in addition to adding his welcome to the group, made the announcement that the road that ran through the heart of Berryville and where most businesses in the area were situated, would no longer be only referred to as CR 4117, but also as "Mattie Albright Road," with street signs declaring as such. Those signs had been in place for a couple of days prior to the meeting, unbeknownst to Mom and Dad and most of the citizenry. I happened to be sitting next to mom when Oris made his announcement, and like I did when I became aware of the road naming, she choked with emotion, and I witnessed a silence on her part that was very rarely seen. She was out of words as Oris presented her with another plaque that included a picture of one of the street signs with her name. Dad had not yet gotten over the surprise arrival of Gerald and me, but he was now totally shocked and stunned at the news. He was beaming with pride about Mom, and later declared that the Albright name would last for a very long time in the East Texas area where he was born and raised. In addition to Mom having a road named after her, his name is on the cornerstone of the Mt. Olive Cemetery, where he and Mom would eventually be buried. He served on the board as vice president when the graveyard was being cleaned up and enhanced to provide a more pleasant environment for the deceased. Additionally, the name of Dad's father, George Albright, is included on the corner stone of the Mt. Olive Sand Flat Baptist Church for serving as a trustee for the church and assisting with its renovation.

Following the council meeting, Mom, Dad, Gerald, and I went to the Berryville home, and had some coffee and cake that Mom had baked, as if the reception following the meeting hadn't provided us with enough sweets. As usual, Gerald and I took our customary barstool seats at the counter that bordered the kitchen, and mom sat on a stool inside the kitchen facing us. Dad customarily sat at the counter, but this evening he sat in the living room on the sofa twiddling his thumbs. The evening's events had overwhelmed him. He was filled with some mixed emotions. On the one hand he was extremely proud of mom and the honor she received. On the other hand, and over the previous few years, the two of them had many conversations, some unpleasant, about the amount of time she was spending in her civic and charitable activities. While he was sitting on the sofa it became clear to me that he was experiencing some guilt feelings about those conversations. I approached and re-minded him that the name of the street signs in Berryville was not "Mattie Dabner Road" but rather "Mattie Albright Road"—it was his last name on the signs near the town where he was born and raised. He looked up at me, smiled, and remarked, "I knew who I was marrying sixty years ago." We all laughed, Dad's guilt feelings eased, and he joined us at the kitchen counter for some cake and coffee. It was fortunate that Dad was in attendance at the council meeting to witness Mom receiving the historic honor of having a street named after her. He passed away four months later on 8 September 2003.

The rare occurrence of naming a road after an individual is an honor that would not only be appreciated and cherished by the honoree, and his or her family and friends, but also by the officials who decided to take this action, and hopefully the citizens in the community where the road resides. Many who will see the Mattie Albright Road street signs will wonder why this historical action was taken by the Berryville City Council. This book answers this question based on interviews conducted with a number of individuals in this East Texas area with whom Mom worked and collaborated. Equally important, the book presents her history, education, and family life that laid the foundation for the contributions she made to the communities in which she lived.

Berryville honors retired leaders

Citizen Photo

Mattie Albright Road
The City of Berryville has named County Road 4117 the "Mattie Albright Road" in honor of longtime civic leader and Council member Mattie Albright.

SENIOR NEWS LINE

By MATILDA CHARLES

It's a good thing I respect my teeth, otherwise I'd be gnashing them down to the gum line after attending a seminar on aging, and hearing one of the experts say that the best way to forget that we're getting older is to shop

Frankston Citizen Photo

Retired Council members honored
The City of Berryville Tuesday night, May 6 honored Mattie Albright and Grace Donnelly for their many years of service to the City of Berryville with a reception at the Berry Community Center after the Berryville City Council meeting. In addition it was announced that County Road 4117 will be named in honor of Mrs. Albright. In front from left are W.D. Albright and Mrs. Albright. Standing, from left, are Grace Donnelly and Mayor James Calvin. Both honorees served many years on the Berryville City Council before they retired recently.

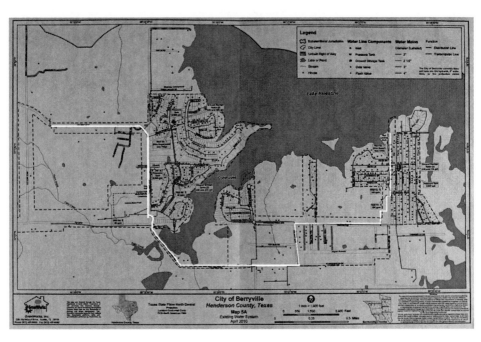

City of Berryville with Mattie Albright Road Outlined in White

The Albrights at the Dedication of Mattie Albright Road—May 6, 2003

The Berryville City Council Honoring Mattie P. Albright and Grace Donnelly — May 6, 2003

Epilogue

**Where is that hero to regenerate our pride
And on whose shoulders we can depend?
That special hero is not special at all
That hero resides deep within**

Excerpt from "The Hero Deep Within"
Copyright © 1991 by William D. Albright

On March 18, 2006, sunset levied its inevitability on the life of Mattie Pearl Albright. She was eighty-eight years of age and tired, and while her mind was keen and shrewd, her body had been deteriorating for some time and finally gave out. Following the death of Dad in 2003, Mom greatly missed her life partner; she kept a copy of his obituary on her nightstand and kissed it every night following her prayers. Given her health, she wished to join him, as she rarely left the house, and when she did, it was to visit her doctors. Her wish was granted on March 18th and her funeral was held on March 25th at Frankston High School, since her place of worship, Mt. Olive Sand Flat Baptist Church, was too small to accommodate the anticipated crowd of attendees. Half of the auditorium at the high school was filled and the attendees were very diverse—young and old, black and white, white- and blue-collar workers, farmers and ranchers, and businesspersons. The audience was clearly representative of the population impacted by Mom's influence and efforts, and the pallbearers, both black and white, included family members and colleagues with whom she worked on the chambers and the city council. Rev. S. Douglas Turk, pastor of Mt. Olive, officiated at the services with the assistance of Rev. Mellie Arps of Tyler, Texas who also presided over the 50th anniversary during which Mom and Dad renewed their vows. Rev. Arps remarked during the funeral services that "Mattie was a powerful and determined woman, and she is now giving Dub plenty to do up in heaven." Mom's funeral was administered under the direction of Mercy/McGowan Funeral Home of Jacksonville, TX. The original mortuary, Mercy Funeral Home, was founded by Ernest Cantley, a brother to my Grandmother Mozell, and was named for his wife Mercedes. Ronnie McGowan worked at the mortuary for Mercedes, after Uncle Ernest's death, and took over the establishment following her death in 1990. The funeral home has directed the services of most of the Albright/Cantley family members residing in the East Texas area. And now the staff was professionally taking care of Mom's services.

The funeral was a mixture of emotion ranging from sadness resulting from knowing that her presence would definitely be missed to pride for what she contributed to the community and individual lives. I delivered a tribute to her that attempted to capture this range of sentiment and my personal reflections on the various roles she played as a mother, mentor, role model, comforter and healer. In part, my remarks were the following: "The dictionary defines a Mother as 'a woman who conceives, gives birth to, or raises and nurtures a child; a woman who shows maternal love and tenderness; a female ancestor;

a woman who holds a position of authority or responsibility; a woman who creates, originates or founds something. The word Mother is used as a title for a woman respected for her wisdom and age.' Ladies and gentlemen, I believe that I have just defined Mattie Pearl Albright in the truest and purest sense of the word. First, she gave birth to four children. After losing two following their birth, she raised and nurtured Gerald and me. She gave tremendous love, compassion, wisdom, and protection to the two of us. She passed this same love, compassion, and protection on to her grandchildren and great-grandchildren, knowing that her legacy was passing through the veins and minds of her wonderful descendants."

"Next, she was a woman who came to live in what ended up being her final home, Frankston/Berryville, Texas. Let me add, however, that she came to this part of the country with much hesitation, having spent thirty-two years in Los Angeles. But she came to this area to be with her love, our father, in his birthplace, and to prove once again the truth in the old adage that 'home is where your heart is.' She was a leader, bridge maker, a giver to the poor and young, a friend, mentor, and one who would give you a piece of her mind, as I know many of you received. But what a wonderful piece it was, and she was usually correct.

The beautiful thing is that this community embraced the character of Mattie Pearl Albright, not only in accepting her as an individual, presenting her with awards for her efforts, but also in the love and friendship that many individuals gave her. And on top of this, the community bestowed upon mom the ultimate recognition, the designation of County Road 4117 as Mattie Albright Road, a distinction that very few individuals receive anywhere. Mom's roots and influence run deep not only within her wonderful family, but also within this community that she came to love and cherish. Indeed, she was a mother to the community." This tribute was followed by a tremendous rendition of "Amazing Grace" performed by Gerald on his saxophone.

When the family exited the auditorium to proceed to the interment, we were astonished to realize that the funeral procession would be led by official civic components of the Berryville and Frankston communities. Leading the hearse, funeral cars with family members, and the many other followers were several police cars and two fire trucks. Mom had served as a director of the Berryville Fire Department. They led the procession north on Route 155 for about two miles and made a right turn on Mattie Albright Road. The family marveled at the street sign with Mom's name as we made that turn and the other signs we saw as the procession continued down the road. Mom was travelling down part of a 5.5-mile stretch of road pavement named after her on the way to her final resting place next to Dad at the Mt. Olive Cemetery.

Many heroes and heroines live their lives without much notoriety and are essentially unknown to many. We do not know their names though their contributions to family, community, city, state, or nation may have been significant. In the case of Mom, her name is known not only by those she touched over her lifetime, but also because the Berryville City Council determined that her overall contributions to the area-wide community were worthy of informing all who drove down the road that significant and transformative achievements had been made by the individual after whom it is named. The East Texas area of Frankston, Berryville, Lake Palestine, and Tyler is standing on the shoulders of the "Pearl" called Mattie.

DAD AS VICE PRESIDENT OF COMMITTEE TO UPGRADE THE MOUNT OLIVE CEMETERY

MOM AND DAD AT REST IN THE MOUNT OLIVE CEMETERY

Mattie Pearl Albright—circa 1988

Acknowledgements

1. Interviews for the book
   a. John F. Berry—Attorney-at-Law
   b. Raymond Blevins—Certified Public Accountant
   c. Lillie Claybon—Former Member of the Berryville and Lake Palestine Chambers of Commerce
   d. James Colvin—Former Mayor of Berryville, TX and President of the Lake Palestine Area Chamber of Commerce
   e. Susie Lyles Dabner—Sister-in-Law to Mattie P. Albright
   f. Grace Donnelly—Member of Berryville City Council
   g. Sharyn Harrison—Manager, City of Berryville
   h. Tony Herrington—Owner of the Coffee Landing Restaurant, Coffee City, Texas
   i. Bob Pickle—Former Constable of Poynor, TX and Board Member of the Berryville Chamber of Commerce
   j. Joe Tindel—Former Owner of the Frankston Citizen Newspaper
   k. Belinda Wallace—Teacher, Poynor Elementary and Middle School
2. Literary Sources
   a. The Great Migration: Creating a New Black Identity in Los Angeles by Kelly Simpson
   b. History of Shreveport—Wikipedia
   c. Caddo Indians—www.caddohistory.com/caddo_indians.html
   d. Berryville, Texas—Texas State Historical Association—www.tshaonline.org
   e. Frankston, Texas—Wikipedia.org
   f. Berryville, Texas—Wikipedia.org
   g. Anderson County, Texas—East Texas Genealogical Society
   h. Anderson County, Texas—Wikipedia.org
   i. Anderson County, Texas—Texas State Historical Association—www.tshaonline.org

   j.   Lake Palestine—Lakepalestinechamber.com
   k.   Lake Palestine—Texas State Historical Association—<u>www.tshaon-line.org</u>
   l.   History of Frankston, Texas writing by Quanah Price and Reagan Jones
   m.   Top Ladies of Distinction—<u>www.tlodinc.org</u>
   n.   A Brief History of Pearls: How Pearls form in the Oyster—<u>http://www.americanpearl.com/historyoyster.html</u>
3.   Photographic Support
   a.   Ashleigh Bing
   b.   Glenwood Jackson Photography
   c.   LaShawn Kelly
4.   Genealogical Support
   a.   Debbie Montgomerie

CPSIA information can be obtained at www.ICGtesting.com
Printed in the USA
BVOW02*1655221115

427501BV00001B/2/P